T0132131

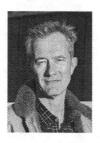

GEOFF DYER

'Broadsword Calling Danny Boy'

Geoff Dyer is the award-winning author of many books, including *But Beautiful, Out of Sheer Rage, Zona* (on Andrei Tarkovsky's film *Stalker*), and the essay collection *Otherwise Known as the Human Condition* (winner of a National Book Critics Circle Award for criticism). A fellow of the Royal Society of Literature and a member of the American Academy of Arts and Sciences, Dyer lives in Los Angeles, where he is writer-in-residence at the University of Southern California. His books have been translated into twenty-four languages.

www.geoffdyer.com

ALSO BY GEOFF DYER

GEOFF DYER

'Broadsword Calling Danny Boy'

Watching *Where Eagles Dare*

VINTAGE BOOKS

A Division of Penguin Random House LLC
New York

FIRST VINTAGE BOOKS EDITION, MAY 2020

Copyright © 2018 by Geoff Dyer

All rights reserved. Published in the United States
by Vintage Books, a division of Penguin Random House LLC,
New York. Originally published in hardcover in Great Britain
by Penguin Books, a division of Penguin Random House Limited,
London, in 2018, and subsequently published in the United States
by Pantheon Books, a division of Penguin Random House LLC,
New York, in 2019.

Vintage and colophon are registered
trademarks of Penguin Random House LLC.

The Library of Congress has cataloged the Pantheon edition as follows:
Name: Dyer, Geoff, author.
Title: 'Broadsword calling Danny Boy' : watching Where eagles dare /
Geoff Dyer.
Description: First United States edition. | New York : Pantheon Books,
2019. | Includes bibliographical references (pages 119–121).
Identifiers: LCCN 2018018214
Subject: LCSH: Where eagles dare (motion picture)
Classification: LCC PN1997.W467 D94 2018 | DDC 791.43/72—dc23
LC record available at https://lccn.loc.gov/2018018214

Vintage Books Trade Paperback ISBN: 978-0-525-56308-2
eBook ISBN: 978-1-5247-4758-9

Author photograph © Matt Stuart
Book design by Peter Andersen

www.vintagebooks.com

That idiot movie! Now I find it blessed.

—Max Jacob, 'Christ at the Movies'

Do the mountains and the blue Bavarian twilight cause the drum march to rattle into existence—is the music an emanation of the mountains?—or are the peaks and valleys hauled into view by the march of drums? Are these Heideggerian questions, or is it just that the Teutonic opening credits—as red as the background of a Nazi flag—could not be any redder against the mountainous blue of snow-clad mountains and the deep blue sky passing for night? The wind is blowing through the mountain peaks, howling in that snowy, Alpiney way, and the drums are more strident, more martial, and there are possibly even more of them than there were a few moments earlier, marching in formation, flying. 'We were over Germany, and a blacker, less inviting piece of land I never saw,' writes Martha Gellhorn in *The Face of War*. 'It was covered

I

with snow, there was no light and no sign of human life, but the land itself looked actively hostile.' We feel the same, even if the hostile land is not black—but if it was 'covered with snow' then it probably wouldn't have been black when she soared over it in 1945—so the point that needs to be made is that active hostility can look rather scenic too.

An aerial view from a plane becomes a scenic view *of* the plane, flying in lone formation: seen *and* heard, propelled by full Brucknerian orchestra now, with a howling tailwind and drums marching so powerfully they could invade the soundtrack of a neighbouring cinema. Then it's a view from the plane again, peak-surfing over the snow-scored mountains, tilting and gliding through the mountain passes, affording Panavision views of . . . Where are we exactly? Font-wise, as the credits continue to roll, there's a hint of Castle Dracula and Transylvania—of Christopher Lee and Hammer horror—but the plane is a German plane, a Junkers Ju-52, and it's giving a very persuasive demonstration of not only its manoeuvrability but also the excellence of its camouflage as it blends in with the snowbound night. If a portion of the mountains had sprung to life, broken off and assumed aerodynamic form it would look exactly like the plane that is flying over them as they stretch out like an enormously dormant snow leopard.

The cockpit is greenishly lit, the pilot is wearing heavy gloves—it's cold inside as well as out—and the seven passengers sitting in a row in their snowsuits, Clint Eastwood at one end, Richard Burton at the other, are all looking anxious. Eastwood's way of looking anxious is to look relaxed, confident that the chaps in the middle are looking more anxious than him, which they are, of course. How could they not, relatively speaking, diminished as they must be by the simple fact that they are not Eastwood or Burton while being sandwiched between them? Burton is looking anxious because he has money worries of the kind that people who aren't weighed down by vast quantities of cash cannot begin to understand. Because he has enough dough to burn an elephant, more money than you could ever know what to do with, he has got into the habit of buying so much stuff that he might not have enough money to buy even more stuff. That's one of the motives for doing a picture like this, which will bring in fabulous amounts of money: so that he can buy his modern-day Cleopatra ('money for old rope' was her verdict on this caper) things like a jet with burnished gold thrones instead of seats. Or it could just be that he's nursing a killer hangover (symbolically suggested by the way that, stacked up near him, are what appear to be metal beer barrels), so that as they approach the drop zone he looks at the blinking red light, pulsing like a headache, like a warning of imminent liver failure, and we are suddenly back in the pre-mission briefing room where another red light is flashing—a nice touch by director Brian G. Hutton—as Patrick Wymark (Colonel Turner) gives the briefing as though it's been scripted not by Alistair MacLean but by William Shakespeare.

Pre-mission briefings are always addressed to the audience as well as the actors gathered around to listen, sitting or standing (Eastwood at the back, half in shadow, a shadowy presence), who are effectively our surrogates, eager to know what we and they are in for. Wymark points with his stick to the map on the wall, to the Schloss

Adler, the Castle of the Eagles. Well named, he says, because only an eagle can get in there. He's right, it (the film) is well named in the way that book or movie titles beginning with 'Where' (. . . Angels Fear to Tread . . . the Green Ants Dream) or 'When' (. . . Eight Bells Toll . . . Worlds Collide) or (For) 'Whom' (. . . the Bell Tolls) always are. Where Eagles Dare anticipates the widespread popularity of the SAS motto 'Who Dares Wins,' even though it was made a dozen years before the storming of the Iranian Embassy (1980), of which the film could be seen either as a prophetic allegory or a direct inspiration. And the title is not just a sonorous bit of rhetoric plucked from Shakespeare by producer Elliott Kastner, who needed something better than the 'awful fucking title' MacLean had come up with (Castle of Eagles). Kastner's title cleverly inverts or, as is said in the world of agents and double agents, 'turns' the intended sense of the lines in Richard III: 'The world is grown so bad / That wrens make prey where eagles dare not perch,' words that Burton could have enunciated with the clarity Larry Olivier would later bring to the voice-over of all twenty-six episodes of The

5

World at War, starting with the famous opening shots of Oradour-sur-Glane ('Down this road, on a summer day in 1944, the soldiers came . . .'), a clarity Eastwood neither attempts nor envies, especially since the English officers in the briefing all look like they're kitted out in uniforms from the previous war or a shelved episode of *Dad's Army* while he lounges at the back in something much sharper, more contemporary, more *American*-looking, sporting a post-Elvis haircut and wearing the shoulder flashes, as Wymark points out, of the American Ranger Division. A plane, a de Havilland Mosquito (as featured, a few years previously, in 633 *Squadron,* about another raid on an otherwise *impregnable* target),* crash-landed near the Schloss where one of the plane's passengers has been taken for interrogation. The mission is to get him out. Get him out before he talks, before he starts singing like a canary. The only way to do this is with stealth and secrecy. And you gentlemen,

---

* By the time I was twelve the idea of the *impregnable* had been so thoroughly impregnated by notions of pregnability that to describe a place as *impregnable* was to suggest its extreme vulnerability to infiltration and attack.

Wymark adds with a flourish, are all stealthy and secretive. So stealthy and secretive that none of them betrays the slightest reaction to this rhetorical compliment. The purpose of the mission is now clear—and how could it not be clear when it's all being enunciated with such impeccable clarity? Essentially the briefing is a virtuoso display of syllabic carving, an elocution demo, and given that the film often reflects on what it's up to it's a shame that the word 'enunciate'—couldn't the mission be code-named Operation Enunciate?—is not itself *enunciated* in the course of this briefing, in which Eastwood (Lieutenant Schaffer) is entirely silent even when he's introduced to the others, so although he might be taken as a representative of the new American style of nontheatrical acting he's also a leftover from the silent-movie era.

All of you, Colonel Turner continues, besides being fluent in German, are expert at survival 'behind enemy lines'—a three-word phrase which has never lost its appeal, which still describes the allure and glamour of the special forces, and which exerted such a hold on my childhood that it sometimes seemed that the purpose of *enemy lines* was primarily to afford small teams of highly trained soldiers the chance to go on acting missions and utter their lines behind them. A subset of soldiers who find themselves behind enemy lines are POWs who want to break out of prison, ostensibly to get back to Blighty, in front of enemy lines, but also in order to behave like real soldiers *behind enemy lines:* darting around, evading capture and generally making a nuisance of themselves (Steve McQueen and his motorcycle most spectacularly, in *The Great Escape*), though none will cause as much of a nuisance as this seven-man team, one of whom now feels compelled to enquire—presumably as a representative of potential audience scepticism about the planned mission—why they don't just send in a Pathfinder squadron of Lancasters and blow the Schloss to kingdom come?* Because, replies Michael Hordern (Admiral Rolland), clearly determined not to be out-enunciated by Patrick

---

* The Avro Lancaster was my second-favourite—and the second-most-complex—Airfix model aircraft after the American B-17 'Flying Fortress.'

8

Wymark, the prisoner, General Carnaby, is one of the architects of the Second Front and blowing up the Schloss would involve blowing him up too, thereby threatening the UK-US alliance on which the fate of the world depends. Which means, more immediately, that the fellow who asked the question can only sit there like a kid in a history class who's been given a rap over the knuckles by a teacher whose dedication to the annual production of the school play is a matter of proven record.

So that's it, they've got to get in and get Carnaby out, before he spills the beans on the Second Front. Over and above this possibly impossible mission the larger importance of special operations has been emphatically affirmed. This is in keeping with the way that the role of the Special Operations Executive was 'puffed by a powerful lobby of historians, some of whom were its former officers.' The truth, John Keegan continues, is that the SOE 'largely fails in its claim to have contributed significantly to Hitler's defeat.' It all depends, I suppose, on what is meant by truth. Isn't it true, for example, that when Max Hastings summarizes the hopes of Operation

Biting—a 1942 plan to capture Luftwaffe night-fighter radar systems from Bruneval on the coast of northern France—in his book *The Secret War,* he does so in terms that echo Wymark's? 'Surely it should be possible for a daring raiding party to get in—then, more important, out, having secured priceless booty.'*

Operation Crossbow, The Guns of Navarone, Cockleshell Heroes, The Heroes of Telemark and *The Rat Patrol* enacted the (repeatedly heroic and daring) truth of my boyish perspective on the war. That perspective has since been altered, corrected, radically changed, but nothing can erase it entirely—any more than an acknowledgement of the decisive importance of the Battle of Stalingrad can downgrade the *formative* role of the local Battle (of Britain) or the retreat from Dunkirk in my enduring interest in the Second World War.† And if director Brian

* The comparison is helped by the way that the 'Bruneval raid was the most successful such operation of the war.'
† Christopher Nolan's *Dunkirk* was an overwhelming experience, partly because I saw it on IMAX, as Nolan intended. But also—and perhaps this too was intentional—because it was like witnessing a dramatized, massively

G. Hutton cannot comfortably sit alongside auteurs such as Tarkovsky, Herzog, Antonioni et al., *Where Eagles Dare* still seems, fifty years after its first release, to contain some essence of what cinema means to me now, when action movies have become a form of explosive torpor. 'Every onlooker who fancies his powers of discrimination has a wonderful time when a blockbuster flops on the opening weekend,' writes Clive James in *Cultural Amnesia*:

> But the blockbuster that we actually have a wonderful time watching is a more equivocal case. *Where Eagles Dare* has always been my favourite example: since the day I first saw it, I have taken a sour delight in rebutting pundits who so blithely assume that the obtuseness

_____

enhanced projection of some of the components of the national culture that had formed me and my contemporaries. The film was designed to be immersive; what it immersed me in—symbolically expressed by the Spitfire gliding silently onto the beach where the stuff of consciousness yields to and is cushioned by the claims of the unconscious—was the experience of seeing what was already there, waiting for the film as it landed in my head.

11

onscreen merely reflects the stunted mentalities behind the camera, and I go on seeing its every rerun on television in order to reinforce my stock of telling detail—and, all right, in order to have a wonderful time.

It's not just that I'd rather watch *Where Eagles Dare* than Wim Wenders's *Until the End of the World* because it's more fun; I'd rather watch *Where Eagles Dare* because it's better than *Until the End of the World*—but then, what could be worse?

Before we've had a chance adequately to reflect on such matters—or on the preponderance of *W*s in the preceding sentence—we're back in the plane, which is now over the drop zone. (Since *the drop zone* is almost always *behind enemy lines* it serves as a vertically concentrated essence of the horizontal expanse of generalized danger evoked by the latter term.) They're clipping their parachutes to the static line, the red light is flashing green, and they're tumbling out of the door. First out are the beer barrels, as if the whole mission is really a pretext for a behind-the-lines keg party, except we can see now that they're actually canisters of equipment, bigger and longer than kegs but surprisingly small given the scale of the mayhem their contents will inflict on the host nation. Last out, several seconds after the last of the seven-man stick—and unseen by them—is a woman.

Landing in cushioning snow and trees, the silver canisters have the quality of seasonal hampers stuffed full of guns, explosives and other weaponry—exactly what we wanted for Christmas as kids. After the hamper-canisters come the men, their mushroom canopies drifting slowly and softly over the soft and silent snow in which they land softly and safely, silently and whitely, discreetly, very whitely. It's so idyllically wintery it could be a scene on a Christmas card from jump school. They're behind enemy lines, but there's not an enemy in sight (because the enemy is even deeper behind enemy lines than they are?). One member of the team is missing and they spread out to look for him, trudging through the knee-deep snow, all wearing their snow-patrol parkas and over-trousers.* It doesn't

* One of the most prized items in my Action Man's wardrobe was his ski patrol outfit. I remember it vividly—the green goggles, the oven-glove white mittens that rendered the white rifle unholdable—because my parents bought it

take long to find the missing man. 'Major!' bellows one of the search team, loudly disregarding what might reasonably be assumed is the first rule of stealthy survival behind enemy lines. The missing man is no longer a missing man; he's a dead man. His neck's broken (the snow is not as soft as it seemed), so now there are just six of them. It's a bad start, possibly an ill omen, but missions behind enemy lines have a habit of going wrong: the Black Hawk shot down over the Mog, the attempted rescue of the hostages in Iran that put paid to Jimmy Carter's presidency, the helicopter crash that jeopardized the mission to whack Bin Laden, the discovery of the sniper team by Afghan shepherds in *Lone Survivor* . . . In combat anything that can go wrong will go wrong—at the worst possible moment,

---

for me on an inappropriately sunny day when I had a tooth pulled at the dentist's. On the way home my mum told me off for spitting blood onto the pavement and gave me a handkerchief to spit into. Later she took a picture of my dad and me in our garden, in the sun with our shirts off, while Action Man toiled away conspicuously on the grey grass of the lawn in his white parka and skis like some totemic warning about the looming catastrophe of climate change. That was the nearest we ever got to a skiing holiday.

before the combat, properly speaking, has even begun in this fictive instance. So Burton (Major Smith) doesn't waste time crying over spilt milk—he tells the rest of them to continue unpacking the hampers while he tests the dead man's radio. Makes sense—though as soon as they've trudged off he becomes more interested in the dead man's address book or notebook, which isn't necessarily so weird since it contains much-needed call signals; but the music has turned a little spooky, positively Hitchcockian. There's more to this mission than meets the eye—which becomes more apparent when they get to the cosy, conveniently located Alpine barn and are shuffling off their snowsuits and changing into their German uniforms. This just isn't me, says one of the team, a guy whose name, whether his actual name or that of his character, we haven't even bothered learning, so that we don't know or care whether 'this' (the uniform) is 'me' (him) or anyone else (not him). Burton announces that he can't use the radio because he's left behind the codebook which we've seen him tuck into his own tunic just a few minutes earlier, when they were out in the cold snow, before they got to the cosy cabin. To retrieve the notebook that doesn't need retrieving he trudges out into a blizzard that doesn't look like much of a blizzard, but he only goes round the corner to a neighbouring hut where, rather conveniently, Mary Ure—last seen jumping out of the plane—is waiting in her winter-espionage wardrobe. Without so much as a by-your-leave Burton rummages through her luggage, where he discovers some undercover, lacy underwear, which he holds up admiringly, though to twenty-first-century eyes they seem like bloomers. So far Burton has done nothing but give orders, so this is an important exchange in that he might reveal another side of his character. This side of his character also involves giving lengthy and complicated orders about what to do and where to go, but for Ure it's a definite improvement on getting her head snapped off every time she opened her mouth—or didn't open it—when they played opposite each other as Jimmy and Alison Porter in *Look Back in Anger* ten years earlier. He doesn't even raise his voice while putting her straight after she says she has a right to know what's going on. And he does offer up a useful bit of intel, namely that the radio operator didn't die accidentally in the drop: he was killed, his neck broken after he'd been knocked out. So now, in addition to intrigue (what's Ure doing here?) and mystery (why was the radio operator killed and by whom?), there's also suspense. And love interest (Ure again), which is usually conspicuously absent from MacLean's books. There might be love *interest* but there's no love *time,* so after a quick filmic snog—which might stand in for a roll in the hay, of which there is plenty in this annexe to the main cabin—Burton is on his way out and heading back to the lavishly appointed (relatively speaking) boy's dorm where they're all sleeping. Except for Eastwood, who's walking around in his German uniform as though he's still up late at one of those fancy-dress parties that get members of the royal family in trouble because they haven't twigged that there's more to wearing a German uniform than wearing a German uniform, a fact cleverly or stupidly exploited by the Polish artist Piotr Uklański in his 1998 work *The Nazis,* featuring 164 stills or posters of actors playing the parts of German soldiers (not Nazis necessarily), in-

cluding Eastwood in his current role of Lieutenant Schaffer, even though, strictly speaking,
he's neither a Nazi nor a German soldier but an
American Ranger on his first night out with his
new English pals who, for all he knows, are no
strangers to this kind of politically questionable
costume romp.

There's a bit of snoring in the cabin, but
Eastwood is too alert—in a relaxed sort of
way—to sleep, so he's waited up for Burton like
the concerned parent of a teenage son out on
a date on a snowy New Year's Eve. Checking
his watch in a checking-but-not-overly-anxious
way, he kills time cleaning and disassembling
his Schmeisser submachine gun. The idiom
is no accident. His relationship with time—
killing it—accurately anticipates what will turn
out to be a homicidal relationship with almost
everyone he encounters outside this little cabin.
When Burton comes back in with an implaus-
ible story about meeting a stunning blonde in a
snowstorm Clint squints at him suspiciously,
quizzically, Eastwoodly, all the time applying
lube to his Schmeisser, as if he knows the Major
has been up to something, especially when

Burton—having gone to the trouble of retrieving the codebook from a dead body in the dead of night in the midst of a notional blizzard—gives up trying to contact London after a few seconds and says it can wait till the morning.

There was a slight redundancy in the preceding sentence when I said that Clint *squints* at Burton. Squinting is pretty much the limit of Eastwood's facial range as an actor. Eastwood has basically squinted his way through five decades of superstardom, squinting in a variety of outfits (poncho and tweed jacket, most famously) and in response to a variety of stimuli (guns, chicks, gags; danger, love, humour) in a way that renders him, in facial terms, monosyllabic. Or duosyllabic, since the squint crops up with such regularity as to become the default setting of the Eastwood face, so that *not-squinting*—expressing nothing—becomes expressive of the entire range of human emotions that exist beyond the limits of the squint. In this regard he faces, so to speak, stiff competition from numerous American actors from the 1970s, all vying with each other to see who can do most with least—or least with less. David

Thomson admiringly evokes 'the sculptured Lithuanian rock' of Charles Bronson's face as he dispensed 'monumental violence, always with an expression of geological impassivity.' And whereas the face is usually the main way of identifying a person, in *Point Blank* the face of Lee Marvin (Walker) gives nothing away; it's the way he walks that establishes who he is (which is ontologically synonymous with what he does; he is he who walks). But in terms of the non-manifestation of whatever is going on inside—or, possibly, the clear manifestation of an interior nothingness—Steve McQueen was the master. By comparison with McQueen, Eastwood was the Jim Carrey of his day, a virtuoso gymnast of the visage. I said that Marvin gave nothing away; McQueen does—and gives away—less than nothing. Hence the beautiful redundancy or double negative of his role in *The Cincinnati Kid,* in which he has to enact an ideal of the poker-faced poker player. But it's in *Bullitt* that he took things (logically, the opposite of giving) to another level, even if the nature of that level is, by definition, impossible to discern. In *Bullitt* McQueen's face takes us into a kind of submarine world whereby the oceanic depths of impassivity suggest the dense topography of the Mariana Trench with all the dead weight of multiple atmospheric pressures bearing down on it and him; a case, perhaps, of what Thomas Bernhard calls 'exaggerated understatement.' It helps that McQueen's face has no distinguishing features apart from the eyes; Eastwood is strikingly handsome, gorgeous, but he has that essential ability—especially important when playing the part of a cowboy or gunslinger—to be seen to be gazing into the middle distance even when doing up-close work such as obsessively lubing his Schmeisser. So when he looks up across the table at Burton it's as if he's gazing clear across the horizon, through a blizzard of radio static, into the Welsh valleys of his costar's troubled, booze-addled psyche.

Dawn. A day-for-night-becoming-day dawn in the blue-rinsed snow of the Alpine forest. Eastwood and Burton get their first glimpse of the Schloss, the Schloss Adler, while the rest of the team skulk near the treeline. It looks utterly impregnable, even more so when seen through

binoculars. The chuffing noise of a train pro-
vides a clue to potential ingress, though it turns
out to be a red herring since, in a film that will
feature multiple modes of transportation—
planes, motorbike and sidecar, bus—it's never
put to any use again. It seems even more difficult to get into the Schloss Adler than it is to
the Berghain nightclub in Berlin. Undiscour-
aged, Burton tells Eastwood to get the boys
further back, behind the treeline, while he
attempts to call London on the blower. 'Broadsword calling Danny Boy, Broadsword calling
Danny Boy,' a line so effectively embedded in
the national psyche that, more than forty years
later, it was used as a coded text message during the cover-up of the phone-hacking scandal
at News International. This time Burton gets
through straightaway to Rupert Murdoch—
sorry, I mean Michael Hordern—explaining
that Harrod, the radio operator, has been killed.
The person they are hoping to spring from the
Schloss is called Carnaby which, back then, was
the most fashionable street in London, possibly
the world; the dead radio operator shared his
name with the capital's biggest and most famous

shop. Are these names accidental, or are they code for some kind of psycho-retail geography of the city?

Answering another question of Hordern's, Burton clarifies that Harrod was not killed accidentally, and not by the Germans. This is bad news for his superiors in London, severely jeopardizing the likelihood of accomplishing the mission, though for anyone watching now, in the wake of George W. Bush's premature announcement from the flight deck of the USS *Abraham Lincoln,* 'Mission accomplished' has come to mean the opposite—mission *un*accomplished, mission barely even begun or mission jeopardized—so it doesn't really make much difference. Wymark, in any case, is not unduly concerned, since Burton not only has a sixth sense but a seventh and an eighth as well, though what kind of sense this makes is anyone's guess. Mine is that only Burton stands a chance of figuring out the ensuing tangle of seven or eight plot twists that are still in store.

Eastwood's inscrutable binoculars scan the impregnable Schloss, searching for a way in, his eye drawn at last to the cable car—the gun on the wall, according to Chekhov's famous dictum—which will have the most spectacular part to play of all the means of transportation to be featured, easily surpassing that of the helicopter clattering overhead: an American Bell 47. Since Eastwood and co. flew in on a Junkers why shouldn't the Krauts retaliate by using an American chopper? Because the Bell 47 didn't come into service until 1946. Buzzing in straight from the future, the helicopter is bringing a high-ranking German officer, Reichsmarschall Rosemeyer, to interrogate Carnaby. A guard of honour lines up to meet him as he steps off the bird. Among those waiting to be introduced by Rosemeyer's host, Colonel Kramer, is the blond-haired, dark-uniformed Major Von Hapen (Derren Nesbitt) from the Gestapo, a character of such unrepentant Naziness that he is featured twice in Uklański's *The Nazis*. Rosemeyer eyes him with monocled distaste, possibly because, as a liberal, relatively speaking, he despises the Gestapo and their torture chambers, possibly because, in spite of his Iron Cross, he didn't make it into Uklański's exhibition or book.

Meanwhile, at dusk—even allowing for the fact that it's winter, the day has been stunningly short—the Eagles sneak across the snowy railroad tracks, in the wake of a freight train whose role will not extend beyond this cameo appearance (a sad decline from the recent glory years of *Von Ryan's Express* [1965], starring Frank Sinatra, and *The Train* [1964], with Burt Lancaster). They let themselves into a storage unit where Eastwood and Burton strip off their parkas and pull out greatcoats and caps from their small but apparently bottomless rucksacks. They have not packed lightly, these two; they have enough clothes and equipment to keep the Sherpas on an inter-war Everest expedition employed for much of the climbing season. Working within the confines of a smaller costume budget, the others do what they can, reversing their parkas from snowy-white to wintery camouflage. Thus arrayed, like any bunch of lads on a stag weekend, they head into the village of Werfen for a bit of the old après-ski (minus the skiing), a little apprehensive, naturally, this being their first night out on the streets of the resort. The pitched roofs are laden with snow, the streets are bustling with troops and vehicles, and there's so much parping of horns it sounds like an Alpine equivalent of Cairo.

They choose a tavern at random—we'll try this one behind us, says Burton, though as with most things he says he's not saying but ordering. He tells them to keep their ears open for anything about General Carnaby, but it seems a lame excuse for that which needs no excuse, namely getting into the bar and getting a few down them. It's a cosy place with foaming steins, a really festive Bavarian atmosphere and no obviously anti-Semitic conversation. You can't help thinking what fun it would be to attend a fancy-dress party like this in real life, even though you'd catch hell from the tabloids, especially since the guests include none other than the blond beast Von Hapen, in his medal-bedecked Gestapo costume. For once Burton is not the one doing the ordering; it's Eastwood who orders drinks at the bar, thereby raising the possibility that, for all his swagger, command and much-publicized love of drink and his will-ingness to splash out vast sums of money on diamonds, Burton might be that lowest, most treacherous form of British life: a round-dodger, a conscientious-drink-buying-objector and all-round round-shirker. Even this suspicion only slightly clouds the rest of the group's belief that this is surely the best of all Second World War mission-capers, way better than scaling the cliffs of Navarone, sweating your malarial bollocks off on that ghastly bridge over the River Kwai or waiting for Telly Savalas to flip his sicko lid in *The Dirty Dozen*. A top night seems guaranteed as long as they can keep up their German and not be tricked into letting their conversational guard down, as fatally happened, six years earlier, to Gordon Jackson as he boarded a bus in *The Great Escape* (before enjoying extended small-screen resurrections in *Upstairs Downstairs* and *The Professionals*). This seems unlikely, since they are all, as we learned in the briefing, so fluent in German that it sounds indistinguishable from English. That fluency is casually conveyed by the way Eastwood casually asks for 'two beers' as though he's in a bar in Dodge City or Telluride during the film festival. He feels quite at home, in other words, which is not surprising given that it's essentially a western saloon with chaps in German uniforms instead of chaps. They've only had a couple of sips when Burton leaves Eastwood at the bar, sits down with some German officers, grabs the dirndl-clad waitress and plonks her down on his lap. He whistles a song at her—code!—and whispers (though it's still an order, a *whispered* order) to meet him in the woodshed. He's the kind of man who's always meeting women in some kind of shed. Then he tells her—another order—to slap him across the face, which she does, with some gusto, before flouncing off convincingly. The other German officers at the table are not impressed by this display of grab-ass boorishness, so Burton puts them in their place by telling them that he's Himmler's brother—which roughly translates as saying he's a bigger star than any of them, earns the kind of money a bunch of extras could only dream of and, most important, could drink the lot of them under this very table any night of the week. (That's probably a generous translation in light of the opinion of Germans confided by Burton to his diary the year after the film's release: 'Even when they are at their fat chuckling meerschaum-smoking jolly best I see the jew-baiting death's head under the jiggling flesh and the goose-step and the gas-chambers.')

Back at the bar, he and Eastwood inhale a couple of cognacs before Burton slips off to the woodshed, leaving Eastwood to keep an eye on things, i.e. to squint. But he's not just squinting, he's *squinting in German.* In the woodshed it's not the barmaid waiting for boorish Burton—it's Mary Ure, whom he promptly tells to take off her clothes. She's surprised but not unwilling, ready to obey, maybe even turned on somewhat by his German uniform in a 'Fascinating Fascism,' *Night-Porter*ish way, but he doesn't want to get into her pants, he wants to get her into the castle. Helping Mary off with her boots—though even help comes in the form of an order: give me that boot—he explains that the plane with General Carnaby-Street aboard wasn't shot down, it crash-landed, riddled with bullet holes—British bullets, but a hole is a hole is a hole, he says, in a theatrical triple entendre. And General Carnaby is not really General Carnaby; the person they think is General Carnaby knows no more about the Second Front than Burton knows about the back end—what a shame he didn't say 'side' instead of 'end'—of the moon. By association, then, it's obvious he's got more on his mind than the mission as he helps her take off the other boot and explains that the person being held prisoner is an ex-actor, Cartwright-Jones, probably second-rate, playing the role of General Carnaby. Suddenly things have all got rather meta, especially since it's actually Robert Beatty who's playing the role of the actor (Cartwright-Jones) playing the part of Carnaby-Street. He didn't need to be talked into it, Burton explains, he volunteered—what actor wouldn't? Well, one who didn't have Burton's enormous need for money might have thought twice but, yes, in many ways it's a method actor's dream, an opportunity for immersion in character so total that it's highly likely he'll not make it out of the Schloss alive. As Burton says, it might be a short engagement. A one-night stand, says the ever-hopeful Mary.*

* Turning on the TV and surfing through the channels, I am always happy to stumble across *Where Eagles Dare*. The strange thing is that I always bump into the *same* bit—*this* bit. If it's late and I'm drunk I only watch for ten minutes or so, which means that I've seen the sequence beginning

Someone else is coming in. It's Heidi (Ingrid Pitt), the barmaid, but any hopes that we're in for a Bavarian-themed threesome are quickly dispelled by bossy Burton, who explains that she's going to get Mary into the castle. She's not just a barmaid, she's a top agent and, as Burton says while giving her dirndl-enhanced rack an appreciative leer, what a disguise. A year later, after the publication of *The Female Eunuch*, Heidi might react differently, but for now she beams as if this compliment is the fulfilment of all her ambitions and hopes, as spy, actress and woman. It's been a wonderful interlude, a combination of Frankie Howerd and *Carry On Up the Schloss*, all done in impeccable high-thespian style. Unfortunately, Burton has to leave the chill-out shed with its untapped erotic potential

---

roughly with Burton leaving the bar or Heidi entering the woodshed more times than any other part of the film. Is some hidden order of the world revealed by this statistically improbable outcome? Or is it not so improbable after all? Perhaps transmission of the film has tended to start at a time that increases the chances that I will encounter it at this point. A third alternative is that only this fragment of the film is ever broadcast.

and get back to his mates, who are still pissing it up in the boozer. On the way he comes across a body, looking, at first blush, like a rat-arsed casualty from a special New Year's Eve sequel to *Cardiff After Dark*. On closer inspection it turns out to be one of the team, MacPherson, who looks like he's been killed by a vampire. Once Burton's back in the boozer, Eastwood asks him what's going on, not just in terms of all of this dashing out to woodsheds the whole time but more generally, with members of the team dying mysteriously in the snow, and dying thus around us every day. As Burton begins his sit-rep, Mary enters the bar and is greeted by Heidi, who is glad of the chance to avoid the attentions of Derren in his Gestapo getup. Burton always has other things to occupy his six or eight senses—the mission, the plot, making sure he's never near the bar when his friends' thirsty glasses are close to empty; the blond beast is very happy to have not one but two busty fräuleins to flirt with. Another thing on Burton's mind is the dead team member outside in the snow, but as soon as he gathers the troops to explain this latest twist a bunch of Germans burst into the already-crowded-with-Germans bar and say they're looking for five deserters. Clever, concedes Burton, instantly catching on to the fact that, in a *Macbeth*-like world where nothing is but what is not, this is a ruse for rounding them up without attracting attention. Still, it comes as a surprise when he suggests to the team that they meekly turn themselves in. The mission is not accomplished but it's over—kaput. Forty-five minutes into the movie and they're marched out of the tavern like a firm of hooligans at the Winter Olympics, rounded up and taken to the slammer before things have properly kicked off.

The blond beast's evening, by contrast, is going quite swimmingly as he escorts the two fräuleins, glamorous and cosy in overcoats and *'Allo 'Allo!* berets, to the cable car, into the cable car and up to the castle, the castle with its numerous bedrooms, the rooms with beds in them, beds in which a virile member of the Gestapo can already imagine himself saying things like *'Ja, Lickenschaft!'* to one or, ideally, both of his semi-clothed costars, once they get up there, after they get out of the cable car inching and winching its way to the castle.

33

We watch the cable car ascend as Eastwood and Burton (separated from the other three on the grounds that they're officers) are whisked away in a staff car under armed guard, along icy roads in what might not inappropriately be termed treacherous conditions. The car is swerving on the ice, or maybe it's just that there's a lot of sideways glancing going on in the rearview mirror, in front of the back-projected twilight of the rear window. We know something's going to happen, but all that happens is that Eastwood bends down to tie his shoelaces. Except tying his shoes turns out to be a new form of unarmed combat, so perfectly adapted for use in cramped and vehicular spaces that he shoves one of the guards out of the door of a speeding car that *may* have been swerving slightly but is now swerving all over the place. Shots are fired, and when the car crashes into construction works another of the guards gets catapulted through the windscreen like he's been shot out of a cannon in a public information film about the need to clunk-click every trip. Burton is left looking rumpled, slightly headachey (again, nothing compared with some of the hangovers he's had to wade through), and Eastwood is bent double so that when he gets out of the car and wipes his mouth you could be forgiven for thinking that he's just given Burton a blow job at a calamitous drive-in, something the latter must have been ready for given all the lecherous talk when he was, in jazz parlance, woodshedding with the two fräuleins, and although this was not quite the outcome that he was anticipating, Burton's earlier sentiment—a hole is a hole is a hole—hovers like frosted breath in the icy night, the treacherous *selige Nacht*. Setting a precedent for what's to come, the only people to have died in the crash are Germans. Burton and Eastwood pile these dead bodies back into the car and begin pushing it towards the cliff, Eastwood's Schmeisser dangling from his shoulder and pointing at his crotch, dangerously one might have thought. It's one of the gestural quirks of Eastwood's performance: the Schmeisser is forever dangling or falling from his shoulder in a way that seems incompatible with firearm safety protocol. Is the idea to emphasize an off-the-shoulder, gunslinging quality to Eastwood's character, in contrast (again) to Burton's starchy

British fortitude? They push the car over the cliff and the car dutifully does what it's expected to do in such circumstances—it explodes and bursts into obliging flames: an augur of what's in store for many of the vehicles featured in the next hour and forty-five minutes. MacLean is a masterly plotter, but it's hard to see what's been achieved by this detour except the cheap thrills of a relatively minor crash and an incidental explosion.*

Checking in at the Nazi-themed ski lodge, the fräuleins are given a frosty welcome by the S-and-M-looking receptionist. After she shows them to their quarters the blond beast is at a bit of a loose end, so he holds his gloves in one hand and slaps them loosely into the palm of the other, a casually Nazi-ish gesture suggestive of vaguely Nazi-ish intent. His end's still pretty loose as he focuses on the hotel register on the desk, casually perusing it, perhaps with a view to finding the room in which Mary might at this very moment be undressing, slipping into

---

* There is never a dull moment in *Where Eagles Dare*—in spite of the multiple explosions that punctuate its progress. Explosions in film are always a bore.

something more comfortable. Enter Colonel Kramer, who comes down the stairs and catches him at it, even if it's not clear what the 'it' is at which he's been caught, though it is probably not unrelated to what 'it' meant or did not mean when used by Bill Clinton during the Monica Lewinsky scandal. There follows a little dustup between Colonel Kramer (SS) and the blond beast (Gestapo). Kramer tells him the truth about the five arrests in the village: they weren't deserters, they were British agents. This belated revelation—Derren demands to know why he wasn't informed earlier—generates an extended slanging match as the two German stags rub the velvet off each other's high-ranking antlers, snarling and staring at each other, politely addressing one another as Colonel and Major but doing so in a way that becomes more and more loaded with contempt and derision, both of them obeying Hitler's directive not to retreat an inch, working themselves into a lather of offended Teutonic rectitude, adamant that if Hordern and Wymark could deliver their lines in the pre-mission briefing with a clarity worthy of Shakespeare then they can make this spat sound like a dustup between Goethe and Fichte. Colonel Kramer stomps off, shutting the door behind him as another door opens, the door—a smart little edit—to the room where Mary is staying. Heidi, wearing a Boxing Day dress with holly green and red berry trimmings, shows Mary the various espionage tools she's stored away. If one had the skill, this sequence could be digitally amended so that the accessories stashed away by this original agent provocateur—pistol, binoculars—included a selection of sex toys.

Burton and Eastwood, meanwhile, are somehow back in the shed—did they walk, hitchhike, take a bus?—where they'd stashed *their* manly toys (dynamite, guns, etc.). Burton radios home—'Broadsword calling Danny Boy'—and Hordern takes the call back in smoky Mission Control, somewhere in England, probably not far from Walmington-on-Sea. After bringing Hordern up to date on the latest setbacks, Burton tells him that he'll be effecting entrance within the hour, ignoring Hordern's rather premature order to pull out while he still can. Hordern and Wymark both feel badly about the mission, about the way the Germans have totally *penetrated* MI6. In the midst of all the intrigue about double agents an outbreak of third-form double entendres has been transmitted wirelessly throughout the movie, which is itself rather touching since, as they sink into self-reproach, both Wymark and Hordern say that they're getting too old for this kind of thing. For what kind of thing? Picking up big cheques for a couple of days' work that don't make demands on one's ailing memory in the way that theatrical engagements do? It's a lot sodding easier than flogging your guts out as Lear and Gloucester in rep six nights a week with a matinée on Saturday. That's the other nice thing about this scene: you can sort of see that they're *acting* (in an English, non-Brechtian way), that they—especially Wymark—might not mean everything they're saying.

Having done his Broadsword-calling-Danny-Boy routine, Burton takes a break from loading up the rucksacks to look out of the window and introduce what will become another verbal motif: 'We've got company,' meaning that truckloads of Germans have pulled up outside the woodshed,

39

in a resort that's already overrun with Germans. Open the window, he orders Eastwood, before unveiling the quintessential *Where Eagles Dare* accessory: bunched sticks of explosives with an extendable trip wire that can be wrapped around a nearby pole with lethal effect.

With three rucksacks—Tardis-like given what they will later be seen to contain— Eastwood and Burton clamber out of a hatch at the back of the shed and make their getaway as the Germans enter through the front door. The officer trips the trip wire, triggering this least improvised of EDs. The hut blows up, and soon everything around is blowing up in sympathy and there is chaos everywhere. Eastwood sneaks up behind a guard, stabbing him in the neck with one hand and stifling his cries with the other. Though one thinks nothing of it at the time—and certainly not as the ten-year-old who saw the film immediately upon release—this is a terrible thing to do. Put yourself in the poor German's jackboots. How would you like it if you were standing there, directing traffic, trying to cope with all the explosions and fires, when suddenly you feel a hand clamped around your neck, a knife penetrating your jugular and, seconds later, your life flashing before your eyes and the immense cold of death spreading through you. You wouldn't like it at all, but in this context it barely merits a second glance, though of all the deaths dealt out by Eastwood, this is probably the most horrible. It's water off a duck's back to Eastwood, even if what is felt ('the bucking and shuddering of the victim's body and the warm sticky blood gushing out') and heard ('the final breath hissing out') when making an intimate, commando-style killing like this would burn itself into the murderer's memory with potentially traumatic psychological effects later. The parentheses are not from Alistair MacLean but from Lieutenant Colonel Dave Grossman's book *On Killing,* in which he offers an improvement on or update to Eastwood's technique. Rangers and Green Berets are trained 'to execute a knife kill from the rear by plunging the knife through the lower back and into the kidney. Such a blow is so remarkably painful that its effect is to completely paralyse the victim as he quickly dies, resulting in an extremely silent kill.' Well, useful, as Philip Larkin put it in a different context, to get that learned. Even without the benefit of this more-advanced knowledge, Eastwood's victim dies instantly and silently as the falling snow, possibly deciding, in his dying moments, that there was no point making a fuss and raging against the dying of the light because, as another poet asked in a different schloss, *'Wer, wenn ich schriee, hörte mich denn aus der Engel Ordnungen?'**

Keeping his distance, Burton shoots another guard with a silenced pistol—also in the throat, as it happens—before he and Eastwood make their getaway in a motorcycle and sidecar through a snowy scene in which everything that can blow up is blowing up. With so much going on, blowing up and bursting into flames, no one pays any attention to them as they speed along through the flaming flames, Burton finding it all explosively funny, laughing at the mayhem they've just unleashed (only a fraction of what's to come) as they career out of town on the snow-bordered road and affix more of these trip-wire

* 'Who, if I cried out, would hear me up there in the angelic orders?' (Rilke)

explosives to poles and trees for reasons that, like so much else, are not yet clear.

It's snowing by the time they get back into town and let themselves into what looks like another even bigger woodshed but is actually a garage sheltering yet another mode of transport: a red bus with attached snowplough, the engine of which Eastwood is ordered to check. It works, it starts, it's raring to go and ready to plough, but they don't have time to dilly, to dally, to linger or dilly-dally. Eventful by anyone's standards, the day has barely got going, even though night fell hours ago, when they went to the bar where Burton caused offence, before MacPherson was whacked and the remaining members of the crew got themselves arrested, before the car crash and escape, before everything started blowing up and bursting into flames, and Eastwood and Burton took it upon themselves to start killing people with murderous and silent focus on the throat.

As the three other members of the aborted mission are frogmarched up to the cable car, Eastwood and Burton clamber onto the roof of the terminus—with just one rucksack apiece now—and, as the cable car starts its slow ascent, softly clamber from the roof on to the cowling that joins the car to the cable before clambering down from there, even more softly, onto the roof of the cable car itself so that now they're riding up to the Schloss like eagles perched on the cable car, inside of which are their three arrested comrades. Which means that, after a lot of rather superfluous action, they are almost reunited. Hence, we now realize, the arrest and separation of Eastwood and Burton from the others did have a purpose. If they'd all stuck together there'd have been no way five of them— six including the dead MacPherson—could have softly clambered onto the roof of the cable car, so what seemed like a setback and impediment actually turned out to facilitate what had to happen in order for them to gain ingress to the Schloss (looking like Castle Dracula in the day-for-night), through the tunnels of which Mary is wandering in her fur-trimmed coat, past a German soldier who waits till she has passed by and then—who can blame him?—checks her out. Even though he notices her she continues to flit through the castle unnoticed, just as she stowed away on—and parachuted out of—the plane unnoticed. In this respect she is Brian G. Hutton's onscreen representative. Eastwood, Burton and the rest of the team have been praised as stealthy and secretive, but the two stars are constantly drawing attention to themselves. Even when they're trying to pass unnoticed they are paid vast sums to do so in such a way as to draw attention to the fact that they're passing unnoticed. Hutton's stylistic signature as director lies in the absence of anything that might permit us to recognize him as an *auteur*. Apart from the stuntmen—and -woman—no one connected with the film is more undercover than its director.

Unnoticed, Mary enters a room, a random room that is not random at all because, on throwing open the shutters and looking through her bins, who should she see but Burton and Eastwood—remember what was said about their being conspicuous even when hiding? Crouched on the roof of the cable car, these exponents of parkour *avant la lettre* clamber back up to the cowling they've just clambered down from until they're sitting astride it like

45

a mechanical two-man horse. It's a wonder, frankly, that no one in the cable-car station can see them, perched like sitting star-ducks, so we have to assume that the relatively bright lights of the cable-car station render them invisible in the night as, at exactly the moment the car passes under the angled roof of the cable-car station, they leap from the cowling and onto that angled, snowy and therefore slippery roof, just managing to gain a purchase with their ice axes, though Eastwood's slips clear and he slides down the angled icy roof and his long legs are soon dangling off the edge, in plain view, one would have thought, of everyone in the cable-car station who happened to be looking that way, so it's a good job no one was (preoccupied as they were with taking delivery of the prisoners), before he digs it in again and begins hauling his way, inch by agonizing inch, back up the angled roof. Burton has secured himself by this point and reaches out a gloved hand, exactly as in another roof—or ceiling at any rate, specifically that of the Sistine Chapel—until their gloved hands join and they are once again safe, relatively speaking, in the precariously vertiginous way that will characterize safety for the remainder of the film. From here on safe is synonymous with perilous.

Steps have been cut conveniently into the rock by the side of the entrance to the cable-car station and Burton and Eastwood make their way up these convenient steps while Mary affixes a thin line to a conveniently located beam in the room high above. To this thin line they tie a thin rope and Burton begins climbing it, though frankly this looks far beyond his physical capabilities, especially when the rope passes a deeply indented window, thereby risking exposure to the Germans within—partying, it seems—and, riskier still, obliging him to climb up the rope without planting his legs on the wall of the Schloss for support. It's not just beyond *his* capacities; the rope is so thin I doubt anyone could climb it, but I have a fondness for this sequence because it reminds me of the cover of the first Alistair MacLean book I ever bought: *The Guns of Navarone,* a Fontana paperback with a cover photograph, shot from above, of a soldier in German uniform climbing a cliff high above a foaming swirl of sea.

Burton's pretty creased by the time he clambers through the window and into the welcoming arms of Mary. You're getting too old for these insane missions, she says, and she's right on both counts. The mission really is insane, but while, as an actor, Burton did not always choose wisely, his character may have had little choice in the matter. 'Woe to the officer,' wrote David Bruce of the Office of Strategic Services (OSS), 'who turned down a project because, on its face, it seemed ridiculous.' Burton is wiped out by the climb, even if it had actually been ridiculously easy; hauled up by a crane, he was required only to grimace. ('He had more wires on him than Pinocchio,' recalls his stunt double Alf Joint.) With his feet on the ground again he's soon back to doing what he does best: telling Mary what to do—'fetch me a map of the castle'—though as an indicator of his still-weakened condition he adds an uncharacteristic 'would you?,' so strictly speaking (and by his lights) he's not ordering but asking. Once he's got the map he sets out memorizing directions to wherever it is he's trying to get—in its way as impressive a feat as scaling the walls of the Schloss Adler by a rope of such slender plausibility it seems hard to believe it can bear the weight of any further plot development.

Eastwood comes toiling up after him, asking for a hand as he appears at the window, but Burton feels no obligation to help his younger, fitter co-star in this non-life-threatening situation. With or without his assistance, Eastwood is on the way up, poised to become a living legend— a *living* living legend (as opposed to a 'dead living legend,' as Don DeLillo will term John Wayne), while Burton has an inkling that the high points from now on might well be lower than he thought they were going to be when he was making his way to the top. The attitude he shares with a character in *The Transit of Venus*—he was a star, 'any firmament would do'—will play a part in his waning. Neither of them need mention this, but once Eastwood is safely inside he says something else that's not escaped our attention: Burton sure has a lot of women stashed around this country.

They unpack the rucksack that Burton has hauled up after them, and then, without even refreshing themselves with a glass of water, he and Eastwood set off along the corridors Burton has committed to memory, leaving Mary to clear their stuff away like a mom whose teenage kids have come back from a snowboarding holiday in Aspen.

To blend in on their recon of the castle, Burton smokes a cigarette, while Eastwood steps into the radio room and shoots the radio operator with a silenced pistol (anachronistic-looking in relation to the Second World War, but absolutely of its time in that it's straight out of the sleek arsenal of James Bond movies—*You Only Live Twice, On Her Majesty's Secret Service*—from the late 1960s). Burton, meanwhile, has strolled out into the courtyard, where, speaking of anachronisms, the helicopter is patiently waiting for time to pass so it will not look so conspicuously out of place. Having strolled into the courtyard, Burton strolls up to the two guys standing there and asks for a cigarette. It's a powerful demonstration, in its way, of the addictive power of cigarettes. He's only just had one, and now he wants another right away. But his real motive is to get the pilot into the radio room, where Clint, having shot the operator, is waiting to stab him in the back, presumably in the pain-receptive kidneys, as if in the brief time since he stabbed the guard in the throat he has been able fully to absorb the latest advances in commando stabbing. So far he's stabbed two, shot one and been heavily involved in the deaths of the Germans in the car crash, which he initiated by tying his shoelace. After this there'll be no point counting.

Burton comes in to find Eastwood wiping blood from the knife as blithely as Lady Macbeth ('a little water clears us of this deed') before she goes all PTSD, but for us his very insouciance makes us agree with the actress in Hitchcock's *The Lodger* who observes that it's 'a terrible way to kill a man, with a knife in his back.' Not that it's gratuitous. The pilot had to be killed to make sure Carnaby-Street couldn't be flown out and back to the future by helicopter. This having been accomplished, they resume their recce-camouflaged-as-stroll through the castle's schlossy corridors to find Cartwright-Jones, who is straight-batting Colonel Kramer's politely insistent questioning in a magnificent dining hall. As interrogations go it could hardly be more agreeable, a far cry from getting waterboarded in some CIA-sponsored black site, having your fingernails torn out like Violette Szabo in *Carve Her Name with Pride,* or Eastwood stamping on Scorpio's leg—already in less than perfect shape having a) had a knife stuck in it and b) taken delivery of a bullet from a .44 Magnum—in order to get an answer to the insistently squinted question 'Where's the girl?' in *Dirty Harry.** It never occurs to us to wonder how Burton knew that the interrogation would happen in this Wagnerian hall with a blazing log fire, big wooden table and comfy chairs. But we do wonder why Anselm Kiefer has never attempted an epic painting derived from this scene, something like his *Sulamith,* with its vast, cavernous arches, empty (except for the fire burning in its distant centre) and therefore full of historical significance and echoey with myth. Anyway, there they are, Carnaby and his inter-locutors, smoking, having a civilized chat over

* Given the extent of the damage wilfully inflicted on it by Eastwood, Scorpio's leg makes a quite impressive recovery; he limps for the remainder of the film, but, in the circum-stances, amputation above the knee was the best prognosis he could hope for.

schooners of cognac. Except Carnaby is proving to be a reluctant conversationalist—a bit of a wet blanket, frankly—just saying his name, rank and serial number over and over again, so the highly cultivated Reichsmarschall Rosemeyer, who has presumably beaten around the bush already with a bit of interrogative foreplay concerning the rival merits of *Faust* versus *Doctor Faustus*, really has no choice but to tighten the screw and pass the matter on to Colonel Kramer, who says that they have drugs to make you talk. Cocaine, that famous tongue-loosener? Well, this dinner party has suddenly got even better. If this is the third degree then bring it on, right after the Black Forest gateau. Except no, it's not coke, it's something called . . . Scopalamine? Carnaby-Street sneers good-naturedly, like a real hardcore caner and partier, like William Burroughs in *Drugstore Cowboy*. What's that gonna get you? he wants to know. There are other drugs too, says Kramer, glancing at the multitasking Lieutenant Kernitser, the same woman who'd checked in Heidi earlier. As well as being a receptionist and uniformed dominatrix in the hair-dyed, jet-black style of

goth-punk, she is also, apparently, the autho-
rized dealer at a party which has suddenly
turned rather sinister with the possibility, from
Cartwright-Jones's point of view, of becoming a
major bummer, especially when Kramer takes a
call on his phone about the captured agents who
are to be brought on up—the agents, Cartwright-
Jones realizes, who have been sent to spring him.
He'd been enjoying lording it over the krauts in
the starring role of Carnaby; now he's looking
at spending the rest of the war in rep with minor
roles in *Colditz* or *Stalag Luft III*.

Busy, gorgeous, unflappable Mary, meanwhile, is unloading still more gear—explosives
mainly, from that bottomless rucksack—into
her suitcase and slipping a neat little Jane Bond–
type pistol into her handbag when there's a
knock at the door. It's the blond beast, offering
to show her some Bavarian hospitality in the
form of an armaments room converted into a
charming café, an invitation which anticipates
the future not only of Germany but of many
cities in the western world. The thing about
Mary in this film is that as well as slipping about
unnoticed she's also unfazed. He could have

54

said that he wanted her to star in a Nazi-themed bit of gonzo porn and she'd have been unfazed. He could have said anything and she'd have been as unfazed as Gudrun Ensslin from the RAF (Red Army Faction, not the Royal Air Force) when she walks out with him, leaving behind her Baader-Meinhof stash of explosives, listening to him reminisce—as well as being a Nazi he's showing signs of being a persistent bore—about his time in Düsseldorf where he studied under Bernd and Hilla Becher and was close friends with Andreas Gursky, Candida Höfer and the rest.

Back in the dining hall, the party's really hotting up. The three captured agents—Berkeley, Christiansen and Thomas—are there, enjoying a welcoming drink. Unlike Eastwood and Burton, who have constantly jumped between snowy frying pan and icy fire, this lot have been airlifted straight from the beer hall to the safety of a private drinks party. No wonder C-J is looking distinctly down in the mouth, extremely fazed, as Kramer explains that the agents who had come to rescue him are actually double agents, German spies. So it comes as quite a surprise, given that the situation has changed radically to his disadvantage, that he slips back into character and declares with commendable stoicism that nothing has changed. Meaning, effectively, that he *is* up for the drugs after all, which Lieutenant Kernitser reaches for in her sinister-looking handbag. There they are: works and everything. Now this— needles, hepatitis, AIDS, *Christiane F!*—is not what he's into at all. What a relief that Burton and Eastwood decide that this is the point to quietly crash the party, Schmeissers at the ready. Burton takes control. He's happy to see them all here, enjoying a drink. (You bet he is; he's showing considerable restraint in not grabbing the carafe and necking it in one.) Eastwood's got the table covered, so it's another surprise in what's already a surprise-packed scene when that table is turned and Burton orders him to drop the gun and sit down. We have remarked before on Burton's capacity to give orders, to treat the world as his bitch, but in the whole film no order will have quite the authority of the one that will be repeated several times in the next few minutes. It's just one order comprising two words and two syllables—'Sit down'—but he brings to these two syllables a clarity and emphasis of Hamlet's six ('To be or not to be'). Hamlet is asking a question; Burton is giving orders to be obeyed unquestioningly, so when Eastwood responds with his own abbreviated version of Danish existential doubt—first boiled down to 'What?,' then expanded slightly to 'What the hell?'—Burton simply repeats, 'Sit down.'

We've noticed how Eastwood's gun, his Schmeisser machine gun, has been forever dangling from his shoulder; now, on Burton's orders, it is finally dropped on the ground and kicked away as if it's a kiddy's toy. With the floor to himself, Burton tells Eastwood that he is, in his own idiom, a punk. Nice! He's really giving Eastwood a taste of his own as yet unpatented medicine, anticipating by several years Harry Callahan's term of endearment when he asks the wounded bank robber at the beginning, and Scorpio at the end, of *Dirty Harry* if they feel lucky: 'Well do ya, punk?' Not only is Eastwood a punk, says Burton, he's a second-rate one at that. It's the second time in the film that he's called a fellow actor second-rate, and perhaps this insult came so readily to his lips because Burton knows that in the eyes of posterity, and by the standards of which he was capable, he has himself become second-rate, ending up, in fact, as a kind of second-rate Burton, pulling in big bucks starring in stupid action movies like this* when he could have been doing *Hamlet* or *As You Like It,* both of which contain the words 'sit down,' though in *Hamlet,* to be faithful to the letter of text, it's only Barnardo and Marcellus who say 'sit down'; what Hamlet himself says is 'sit you down' (to his mother, Gertrude). But this is the scene where Burton really gets to hold forth and strut his oratorical stuff. If the Great Hall looks like a theatre set—*An Inspector Calls* in Bavaria—that suits Burton fine since, as Clive James puts it, 'from the beginning to the end of his career on screen he looked exactly like a stage actor projecting to the upper circle.' What follows is practically a soliloquy with occasional,

---

* A frequent source of concern in Burton's *Diaries.* See, for example, 23 October 1971, where, after itemizing all the money he and Taylor have been pulling in, Burton writes: 'I would much prefer, for instance, that E and I won Oscars than that a film should gross like *Eagles* and have no importance at all.'

unwelcome interruptions and questions from the rest of the cast. 'Who are you?' Cartwright-Jones wants to know. I'm not Smith, says Burton, I'm Schmidt, a senior officer in the SS—and this Schmidt has quite a tale to tell. But it's a bit difficult to do justice to this tale, a tale told by the opposite of an idiot, if he's also got to keep watch over everyone, so he asks the Colonel to summon a guard, to make sure he's got the full attention of the captive audience whose confused curiosity is a perfect projection of our own rapt bewilderment.

The blond beast also has a captive audience—of one. He's got Mary in the café—sort of a high-altitude *Bierkeller*—and he's tying her up in knots with contradictory memories about Düsseldorf and the location of the cathedral. Looking a bit nervous—fazed, frankly—she downs her schnapps, claims she's got a headache, admits that she's not been to Düsseldorf for ages, wishes she could suddenly be many years in the future when it would be entirely justifiable, when talking about the Düsseldorf School and New Objectivity, to confuse Thomas Ruff with Thomas Struth, though even as she thinks this

59

she realizes it could be a dangerous conversational thread since it could lead the blond bore
to ask if he could interest her—you will excuse
the pun, fräulein—in a bit of Ruff. At which
point, seeing the possibility of subtly moving
the discussion on while remaining in the world
of art photography, she might ask if he knows
the work of Piotr Uklański, specifically his
piece *The Nazis* . . . No, fräulein, I do not, he will
surely say. Well, that is odd, she replies archly,
turning the tables, regaining her composure
because . . . She pauses, hands him her iPhone,
stroking the screen to show this immense wall
of faces, of uniforms, caps and insignia. Because,
she resumes, there you are, Major. And it's true.
There's no denying it. There's a picture of him as
he is now, in this very role, in this very scene in
fact, at this very moment, in the bottom right-
hand corner (second from right, bottom row),
almost as far away as possible from Eastwood
(top row, first left), who, to repeat, is not a Nazi,
and who actually went to some lengths in *Magnum Force,* the sequel to *Dirty Harry,* to restate
his commitment to the rule of law in the face
of all the evidence to the contrary displayed by

60

the earlier film. Not that there is any shame in being seen in this Nazified company. They're all there: the Jameses (Coburn and Mason in *Cross of Iron*), Max von Sydow, Dennis Hopper, Ralph Fiennes . . . Not to have played a Nazi is almost to be a bit B-list (second-rate, in the words of Burton, who's also featured twice, though not in his role as Schmidt).* It's all about the power of glamour, the glamour of power, making you realize that being an actor is one of the few professions that permits the wearing of a Nazi uniform with impunity. Still, she thinks, better to leave it at that rather than risk flattery turning to provocation by pointing out that he actually crops up in this artwork twice, so Mary takes back her phone, turning it off and leaving Nesbitt with a slightly puzzled look on his face, unsure if this self-referential bit of time travel really took place or if he'd just imagined it as a result of catching a glimpse of his own reflection—black

* Featuring a slightly different image-cast from the original artwork, the book version of *The Nazis* includes a picture of Eastwood from *Where Eagles Dare* with Burton (Smith or Schmidt) in the background, thereby completing an almost hat-trick of appearances.

61

uniform, a chest-load of medals, blond eyes, flesh-coloured lips—in a glass. She thinks she's wriggled off the hook, it's difficult to tell, but at least he's agreed to only one more schnapps before escorting her back to her quarters, clicking his fingers for a drink which—another clever cut, reminiscent of the red-light-in-the-plane to red-light-in-the-briefing-room flashback—Burton is downing back in the Kieferian Great Hall. Now that he's got a bit of alcoholic fire in his belly he's really in his element, ready to embark on what will be a slightly preposterous piece of plot exposition about how the three agents we thought were British agents who it turned out (five minutes ago) were German agents are really British agents after all. He then asks Carnaby to identify himself, to admit that he's Cartwright-Jones. When C-J hesitates, Burton whips out that silenced James Bond pistol from his trousers and shoots the corner off his upholstered chair, right by his shoulder—a bit of vandalism which, in the larger scheme of things, is destined to go unnoticed and unpunished, though symbolically he is perhaps making it clear that he, Burton, is the only person in the room with any right to a chip on his shoulder. The idea of all this is to get the three fake German (i.e., British) agents into the top of the high command of the Wehrmacht, he says, really giving 'Wehrmacht' its full Teutonic pronunciation, once again throwing down the gauntlet to the absent Larry Olivier, setting the standard for adoptive pronunciation Olivier will rise to in the voice-over of *The World at War*. It's incredible, says Colonel Kramer, stating the obvious, but Burton can prove it's true by producing the name of the top-ranked German spy in England whose name these three—if they *are* German agents—would know. As if that's not enough Kramer can call Major Wilhelm Wilner at Kesselring's headquarters in Italy. He's there, sound asleep on a snow-drift of comfy pillows in an ornate bed, sporting some Carnaby Street paisley pyjamas, not unlike the ones worn by Steve McQueen in *Bullitt*. It's Schmidt alright, he confirms in the course of a short bit of telephonic cross-examination and banter. And so, with his i.d. vouched for, Burton proposes that the three captured agents write down the names of all the German agents they know who are working in Britain. At which point something extraordinary happens. Instead of ordering the S-and-M, drug-dealing Kernitser to fetch some pencils he asks if she would be good enough to get some pencils *and notebooks*. Two things might be going on here. First, there is the possibility that Burton has contrived this whole scenario as a way of getting the Germans to reveal the location of that much sought-after resource: the stationery cupboard. Other features of both place and mission are emphasized more spectacularly but the revelation—strictly speaking, the implication—that there is a stationery cupboard even here, in the Schloss Adler, and that people will go to inordinate lengths to get their hands on its contents, is one of the film's most profound and subtly expressed truths. No less subtly, the fact that Burton has *asked* for something must be intended to offer a clue to Eastwood—who has been treated like Burton's bitch for the whole film—that he, Burton, is playing a role, is *acting*. Other acts have been less convincing. Mary's, for example. All that stuff about Uklański has the blond beast thinking that the foxy fräulein might not be quite who she claimed to be, so as soon as he's escorted her back to her quarters—without

even trying to invite himself in for a nightcap—
he gets this look of reawakened suspicion on
his inherently suspicious face and strides off,
determined to get to the bottom of something,
or maybe just seized with the desire to see which
rival actors have played their part in Uklański's
Nazi artwork.

Back in the Great Hall it's now a scene from
a uniformed writing workshop, the three agents
busily submitting to the exercise Burton has set
them: 'Imagine you're a double agent . . .' They're
all concentrating hard, like they're back at school
doing an exam as if their lives depend upon the
result, as I must have done at the exact age that
I was when I first saw this film: the eleven-plus,
the exam which determined whether one would
have the transformative experience of going to
grammar school or be condemned, if one failed,
to attending a secondary modern. The blond
beast is striding past the helicopter in the snow,
making his way to the Great Hall where Burton is giving Eastwood a look, a look that is not
subtle, a look that's actually an order saying,
'Look at that machine gun on the floor and get
ready to pick it up, bitch!' The agent-schoolboys

who've finished their writing exercise hand their exam papers to Burton, who hands them to the invigilating colonel (a kind of internal external examiner) to look through and mark. Now compare them with the names in my notebook, says Burton, the Ryman's notebook from the stationery cupboard of MI6. It's as if he's once again trying to show everyone that he's the biggest star in the class. Their notebooks might have the names of a few minor actors, while his will have people like Marlon Brando, Warren Beatty, Stanley Baker and hellraising pissheads like Ollie Reed and Richard Harris. Plus there'll be Liz Taylor's direct line, of course. No wonder Colonel Kramer is so keen to see it. And no wonder he's disappointed when Burton's notebook turns out to be . . . blank. He's been sold a pup. The look on his face says, 'Another incredible plot twist—I can't believe it!' At that same moment he shouts 'Guard!' but it's already too late because quick-on-the-draw Burton has whipped out his silenced pistol and shot the slow-witted guard, while Eastwood, ever ready to do Burton's bidding, has picked up the Schmeisser. He's taken it hard, being called a punk, but it's maybe put an idea in his head that he'll store away and use, years later, in *Dirty Harry,* along with the same facial expression he'll use in every film and situation after this one.

So, Burton has all the names of all the German spies and their contacts in British intelligence. Mission accomplished! But—remember the USS *Abraham Lincoln*—any celebrations are premature because here comes the blond beast, marching down the stairs, brandishing a Luger, and Eastwood is being told, for the second time in ten minutes, to drop his gun. Burton too. The blond beast is mightily displeased, for many reasons. To put it bluntly, he didn't get down Mary's ski pants. And that goading about *The Nazis* . . . It's one thing to be an actor and pretend to be a Nazi. But actors pretending to be Nazis when they're really American or British soldiers— that really takes the shine off the whole thing, makes it all too meta. So he's brandishing the Luger with some genuine actorly fury.* Even

* I remember how much I loved a toy metal Luger I ordered through the post having seen it advertised in a comic, though I can't now recall which comic it might have been. And it wasn't just a boyish thing. A Luger was, by all

though they'd locked horns previously, Colonel Kramer is so glad to see the blond beast—he's saved the day—that he stands up, only to be shouted straight back down: 'Sit down, Colonel.' It's like a musical composition. Burton introduces the command motif—'Sit down'—and now Nesbitt picks it up, more emphatically, repeating it when the Colonel doesn't obey. Burton, though, is nothing if not unflappable. He and Eastwood, he says, have just uncovered a plan to assassinate the Führer. Unable to face another plot twist so hot on the heels of the last one, Reichsmarschall Rosemeyer explodes, 'This is preposterous!,' standing up as he does so, thereby disobeying the most important command—'Sit down'—which Nesbitt repeats, quietly this time, with a waggle of his brandished Luger. Burton is standing. He's in no

---

accounts, one of the most prized mementoes to be looted by Allied troops from dead or captured Germans. In the TV adaptation of *Band of Brothers* Donald Hoobler is so pleased to get his hands on one that he can't stop playing with it, keeps playing with it until he accidentally shoots himself in the leg, through the femoral artery, and bleeds out.

68

mood to take this challenge to his theatrical authority sitting down and he resumes his spiel about a plot to overthrow the Third Reich. You have to hand it to him, he can improvise a speech at the drop of a hat, which makes you think that he is not being entirely sincere when he says to Eastwood that 'second-rate punk' was the best line he could think of on the spur of the moment. Remember, also, that we suspected the blond beast might be becoming a bit of a bore. In his *Diaries,* Burton is constantly calling people bores—even the tragic diva Maria Callas strikes him as 'a bit of a bore'—and actually concedes that he himself becomes a bore when drunk. So one of his six or seven senses probably alerts him to the fact that a major bore, a crashing bore, has just gate-crashed the party he and Eastwood themselves crashed ten minutes earlier. Continuing to think on his feet, he tells Nesbitt that these notebooks contain the names of all the conspirators involved in a plot to kill Hitler. He moves to hand them to the blond bore, passing in front of Eastwood as he does so. At exactly that moment, the moment of maximum danger, Mary opens the door, momentarily distracting Nesbitt, filling his head with a confused tangle of thoughts: Düsseldorf, Uklański, missed pussy. That's all the time Eastwood and Burton need. Like the non-serving partner in doubles tennis, Burton steps aside so that Eastwood can draw his pistol and ace Nesbitt, right in the middle of his thought-tormented forehead. Kramer rises to challenge, so he's shot too, followed by Rosemeyer and the S-and-M dealer who trots towards Mary—in the hope, presumably, of some kind of sorority—so that she is shot in the back, by Eastwood, from behind Burton's back. He's shot them all, all four of them, with the pistol and the aptly named silencer. In the original script the dialogue was shared between him and Burton, but it was decided that Burton could do all the talking and leave the shooting to Eastwood.* When he shoots Kernitser in the back, blood spurts

* The tavern scene in Quentin Tarantino's *Inglourious Basterds* (2009), in which suspicions are raised about Michael Fassbender's German accent, contains multiple nods to *Where Eagles Dare,* climaxing with the shoot-out and its visual allusions to the murderous cool displayed by Eastwood in this sequence.

out of her as if a red faucet has been turned on. I loved that as a kid, as I loved the bit in *Battle of Britain* when a pilot gets shot in the eyes and his goggles turn to blood, but now I find myself thinking that it would have been better if Mary had shot her instead.

Suddenly it's just the original cast of agents who parachuted into the picture in the first place, minus the two who died, plus C-J, who has now risen in the pecking order. As if to show that the subterfuge is over, that this is for real, Burton reverts to barking orders, with none of the 'if you'd be so good as' which struck everyone as out of character. Oh, yes, he's properly back in character now. It's *Mary, bring that back over here,* and, to the three spies, *Put your hands up.* You're late, he tells Mary. One day I won't come at all, she says—the last double entendre of the film. No more of that, as Burton had declaimed when he blacked up for the role of Othello in 1956. From now on, there'll be no time for this Benny Hill / Frankie Howerd stuff because they need to make their getaway. We've got to create enough confusion to get out of here, says Burton. Right now, Eastwood says, he's as confused as he's ever going to be. He's speaking for the audience, but not with the outraged, this-is-an-insult-to-my-Kantian-intelligence of the now-dead colonel. Actually, the now-dead colonel probably overreacted (understandably, since the latest plot twist announced by Burton led fatally to his nonparticipation in any further ones); to be able to dream up these switchback turns and reversals is an amazing ability and it (the plot) does make a sort of far-fetched sense—except for the decision to take along the prisoners, who are obviously going to slow things down (especially with their hands tied behind their backs by Cartwright-Jones) and cause no end of trouble in the course of *the getaway*.

That's what the rest of the film will be devoted to. Sam Peckinpah's 1972 film *The Getaway* (based on Jim Thompson's novel of that name) explicitly declared that the getaway was a distinct entity within the more generic category of 'thriller.' The getaway is the flipside of the hunt, and a significant portion of cinematic history is either the hunt (where your sympathies are on the side of the hunter) or the getaway (when you are on the side of the hunted or the prey), though this rather simple breakdown breaks down with Thomas Vinterberg's *The Hunt* (2012), in which our sympathies are entirely with the hunted, Mads Mikkelsen, who is unfairly accused of being a nonce. Films combining hunt *and* getaway constitute a *chase* (a slow and epic example being Peckinpah's *Pat Garrett and Billy the Kid*), in which it's not always possible to tell hunter from hunted, who is in pursuit of whom. In Michael Mann's *Heat* (1995) Al Pacino is hunting Robert De Niro, but it's De Niro who keeps setting traps for Pacino in order to facilitate his getaway.* The most elemental getaway film is *The*

* The idea of the getaway is the defining factor of De Niro's existence. He's so obsessed with getting away, of being able to leave everything behind in thirty seconds flat, that he doesn't even have anything to leave behind; his house is as empty as the ocean it overlooks. De Niro never hesitates to tell anyone who will listen that he will not hesitate. To do what? To tell people that he will not hesitate. Predictably enough, he then spends the rest of the film *hesitating*. As happened with Hamlet and the obsession with revenge, the idea of the getaway has taken up permanent residence in De Niro's head to the extent that it renders him incapable of getting anywhere. He is constantly getting away from the practical business of getting away. Things start to

73

Naked Prey (1965), directed by and starring Cornel Wilde as the leader of a safari in Africa who is captured by savages. It was derived from the true-life adventure of John Colter, an American scout who was captured by Blackfoot Indians in 1809. They released Colter, naked, and allowed him to run a certain distance before giving chase. In *The Naked Prey* Wilde is permitted to get as far as an arrow shot from a bow before his captors pursue him. Cleverly, Wilde jogs to warm up and only begins to sprint after he reaches that arrow. But in reducing the getaway to elementals in this way *The Naked Prey* violates the essential enacted lesson of the getaway, which is that it should ideally involve multiple forms of transport or at least, in the case of *The Italian Job* (released a year after *Where Eagles Dare*), multiple permutations of the same form of transport—Mini Coopers plus, at the very end, a coach. In *The Getaway* McQueen and Ali MacGraw are reduced to riding in the back of

---

go wrong when the guy he's about to execute—because he's jeopardizing the gang's ability to get away with their latest score—*gets away.* He saw his chance and, unlike De Niro, did not hesitate.

a garbage truck. If *Where Eagles Dare* belongs in the pantheon of great getaway films, that is partly because of the impressive number of modes of transport deployed.

The first stage of the getaway involves the pedestrian business of Brexiting the Schloss. While Burton, C-J and Mary lead away the tied-up prisoners, Eastwood stays behind to wrap more of those trip-wire dynamite clusters around the pillars of the Great Hall. Undramatic and relatively unimportant in itself, this scene is the silent equivalent of a monologue, a wordless soliloquy in which certain key things about Eastwood are clarified. Extremely good-looking, he was perhaps never better-looking than in *Where Eagles Dare.* His hair is cool,* he looks tall and lithe in his uniform as he goes about the business of affixing explosives and, in the process, offers us a masterclass in the art of movement. Actors are expected to exteriorize

---

* Clive James makes much of the fact that Burton 'has gone into action sporting a pageboy hairstyle so fulsome that it spills abundant curls and waves below the back of his collar' but Clint's hair, while tighter at the back and sides, is more rock 'n' roll, more coolly anachronistic.

emotion in the way that Casey Affleck did to Oscar-winning effect in *Manchester by the Sea* (2016), but David Thomson, in the entry on Fred Astaire in his *New Biographical Dictionary of Film,* reminds us of 'a vital principle: that it is often preferable to have a movie actor who moves well to one who "understands" the part.' In the case of *Where Eagles Dare,* there's not much to understand about the part (Eastwood's already expressed his problems with understanding the plot) so that gives him plenty of room for manoeuvring himself around the Schloss with lethal effect. In support of his claim about the importance of movement Thomson cites the 'lounging freedom' of Bogart in *The Big Sleep,* a point echoed by Burton in a documentary about Eastwood, when he draws attention to Eastwood's 'dynamic lethargy.' So here he is, on his own, entirely unconcerned about being left behind, *moving around* the Great Hall with the unhurried grace of Roger Federer in a German uniform, with a Schmeisser machine gun rather than a Wilson racket. As with Federer, Eastwood inhabits a relation to time slightly different from that of everyone around him.

They rush, scramble and panic, while he swans around, rigging the Great Hall with explosives as though setting the table for a leisurely dinner that might be served sometime in the next four or five days.

He then lugs his suitcase full of dynamite to an office of indeterminate function (there is a Kafkaesque quality to the Schloss), except he doesn't really *lug* it because, just as he exists in his own more expansive realm of time, so his personal gravity operates as a fraction of the force that causes the rest of us to lug ourselves around the planet. Our legs may feel like they're made of lead, but Eastwood's suitcase is filled with helium; it floats in his hand before he lays it on the desk of the two Germans working in what looks like a kind of inside-out jail. He says hello, shoots the two Germans—ah, so that was the room's function; it was the *Plötzlicher-Tod-Büro* or office-of-sudden-death—and leaves behind a dynamite cluster as a parting gift.

Burton and the rest creep through the stone corridors of the Schloss until they come to a Second World War equivalent of the DJ booth: a radio room stacked high with equipment where the operator, DJ Adler, instead of sending out Enigma-coded messages throughout the Reich, is playing a little 1940s Lili Marleen–style chill-out tune. Still dynamically lethargic, Eastwood opens a window and lobs a six-pack of dynamite into the anti-aircraft emplacement and then, still holding his ultralightweight suitcase, starts drifting towards the music that is drifting sleepily through the Schloss. When Eastwood catches up with the others, Burton indicates to him that he needs to take care of DJ Adler, who, as well as playing this not-properly-tuned music, is flicking through a book of photographs—by August Sander, even though he had, by then, been banned by the Nazis?—and it's all a bit odd, because it seems he's not broadcasting this music to the troops, he's just using all this high-powered kit to idle away his time, of which he has precious little left because he suddenly hears Eastwood creaking towards him, knife in hand. When he quite reasonably hits the alarm bell, Burton shoots him in the back with his silenced pistol—which he could have done without waiting for Eastwood to creep up and stab the DJ.

Somehow a very tangled-up remix of 'Last

Night a DJ Saved My Life' has been enacted before our eyes, but there is no time to fathom the full implications of what's happened because the castle is all alarums and sirens, and every able-bodied German in the joint is grabbing a gun and the whole place is going into high-alert lockdown even though, strictly speaking, no one knows what the problem is and so they're all running around for the sake of running around.

One person not running is Eastwood, whose Thermopylae-like job will be to serve as bouncer in a cold and clangy corridor and deny all Germans admission to the club where Burton is settling in to the DJ booth—'Big shout going out to the Port Talbot massive!'—to send out his anthemic call sign, so deeply embedded in our consciousness that it actually sounds like he's sampling himself, or doing a kind of backwards sample which involves creating the original from which the sample will later be made, namely 'Broadsword calling Danny Boy.' Desperate to get into the club, the first Germans are clattering up the narrow staircase, Indian file, as they say. Eastwood says to Burton, 'We've got company,' and Burton, instead of replying, repeats his call sign, 'Broadsword calling Danny Boy.' They're like two star saxophonists in a duet, trading signature licks, and it's a shame no one used this exchange in a tune, maybe with a beat derived from Ron Goodwin's soundtrack which, in a few moments, will make an unexpected and distinctly partisan reprise. As the Germans advance along the corridor, Eastwood opens fire, killing the first batch but then having to take cover as reinforcements arrive. They keep him pinned behind the wall, but he still manages to waste some of them by sticking his gun out and firing blind (spray and pray, as U.S. Marines will say of the ferociously committed if untrained insurgents in Iraq) until the hail of bullets, the ricochets, and the concrete-damaging fire become overwhelming and he has to reload.

How does he survive such an assault? Clive James's answer is that, while Eastwood is using live ammunition, the Germans are bound by a long-standing, Geneva-style filmic convention that limits them to 'a special kind of bullet that goes around, instead of through, the actors on our side.' But at this particular moment

Eastwood is also the beneficiary of musical reinforcement. The German firing is intense and rhythmic, but not *disinterestedly* so. For a brief interlude it echoes the percussive theme tune, which heroically returns at moments of high drama. This music is implicitly on the side of the Eagles, so that by performing it with an ensemble of light weaponry the Germans are effectively contributing to their own demise. Every bullet in this rhythmic pattern is a self-inflicted wound. Perhaps that's why they change their tune and bring up a heavy machine gun so fearsome as to make Eastwood *flinch*. Flinching is not a gesture that comes readily to him. He's adept at squinting, might survive a lynching (in *Hang 'em High*), but he don't care for flinching (the radio, let's assume, is broadcasting a little sympathetic hip-hop at this moment), so it's a good thing that the explosives he'd laid earlier live up to their name and start to explode, distracting the machine-gun crew so that he can, with unflinching resolve, emerge from hiding and let loose with an apparently recoil-less Schmeisser in each hand and finish them off, as DJ Broadsword finally manages to summon up Danny Boy on the radio. He only has time to tell him that they've got what they came for and need transport (i.e., they need to make their getaway) before communications are cut and the Germans toss a grenade—a potato masher—at Eastwood's feet. His altered relation to time here proves crucial. They threw the potato masher expecting it to explode within a second of landing. But in Eastwood time that single second expands to five or six, giving him ample opportunity to bend down at his leisure, pick it up and toss it back at them, whereupon it is more than ready to blow up in their faces. When two more land he retreats into the room and locks the door behind him, making us aware of two things simultaneously. First, that the Schloss is one of those places with very low doorways so that there is always a danger— easily overlooked in the face of the other rapidly accumulating sources of harm—of banging one's head. Second, that the getaway necessarily has elements in common with a retreat. A getaway is not just about speed; like a retreat it also involves putting obstacles in the path of your pursuers, in this case the first of a series of sturdy doors and—naturally—more of those explosively effective six-packs.

Burton orders the first of the prisoners, Thomas, out of the side room or walk-in closet into which he'd ordered everyone a few minutes earlier and tells him to climb out of the radio-room window, down the rope he's just attached. Thomas is reluctant for several reasons, one of which is that it's bitterly cold and—diddums!—he hasn't got any gloves. Another reason, of which he is unaware, is that Burton and the others aren't coming with him. They're back in the closet from which he was recently and reluctantly outed. When the Germans come in and find the taut and quivering rope they head straight to the window, see someone making what is presumed to be a getaway and let loose with a burst of Schmeisser fire, whereupon his benumbed hands let go of the rope and the double agent plunges to a double death. More explosions, this time from the antiaircraft emplacement, further distract the Germans and they head off, leaving Burton and the others to emerge from the closet again (the getaway, at this point, involves little more than getting in and out of the closet), retrieve the rope and head back to the corpse-strewn corridors of the castle from which they are desperately seeking egress. Rounds from the antiaircraft emplacement are cooking off, there are fires everywhere and it really does seem that, as Burton intended, the castle is under attack from all directions. In his own small way he has followed Churchill's desire to 'set Europe ablaze.' They sneak downstairs, through the stone corridors and down more stairs, Burton bringing up the rear, shutting a heavy door behind them—but not quite quickly enough as he gets shot in the hand by arriving Germans. With his other hand he is able to tie an aptly named handkerchief around the injured hand. I say injured, but it's not even what used to be called 'a flesh wound'—which typically took place in the shoulder, upper arm or waist—and will not significantly impact his ability to boss anyone around. Elaine Scarry's pronouncement in *The Body in Pain*—'The main purpose and outcome of war is injuring'—is comprehensively refuted by *Where Eagles Dare*. If you're on the right side, the outcome of war is a flesh wound, a scratch. In real life an injury to the hand, with its multitude of little bones and tendons, is a real blow. In a documentary about drug dealers a gang member recounted how his hands 'swolled up' after they were smashed with a hammer when he was suspected of snitching. Even in the realm of fiction, catching a baseball without a mitt causes the hand of the narrator of Richard Ford's *Independence Day* 'to swell up like a tomato'; but the bullet in this Richard's unswolled hand has inflicted roughly the damage that might result from playing with a kitten.

There follows a moment of low-key slapstick—so low-key as to be almost imperceptible—as Cartwright-Jones, following Burton's order to get the men untied and to put on winter outfits, puts his pistol in his coat pocket and misses the target. It takes two attempts to get his gun back in the holster, which is not even a holster, just an overcoat pocket. Imagine Eastwood doing that! Maybe it was a mistake Hutton thought added a sense of human fallibility to offset and enhance Eastwood's implacable cool as he fixes a rope and chucks it out of the window. It's the same thin white rope they climbed up, too thin, surely, for anyone to get a reasonable grip on—especially Burton with his fucked-up, fully functioning hand—but this is not really relevant, as Eastwood abseils down it with that long-limbed easy elegance that could only be his (i.e., his stunt double, Eddie Powell).

Meanwhile, the Germans in the castle have come to the Great Hall, which looks like the castle of Elsinore at the end of Act V: bodies everywhere, including that of Derren Nesbitt, looking very Hamlet-like with his blond hair. But no choir of angels will be singing this Nazi punk to his rest. The investigating Germans open the door, which pulls the cord on the explosives, and soon the whole room is exploding and falling down around them.

The escapers, the getawayers, meanwhile, are on a narrow ledge above the sloping roof of the cable car. It is extremely slippery. I really like this about *Where Eagles Dare,* the way that every sequence, even one which involves relatively little threat, is imbued with danger. All they're doing is walking along a ledge. It's a transitional passage to the next moment of extreme danger but, by any reasonable standard, it's so precarious, so rich in potential for death and injury, that simply being there contravenes multiple health and safety regulations.

The cable-car terminal, now that it's (inexplicably) deserted, looks like the set of a space station, abandoned since the final episode of *Dan Dare* was filmed here years earlier and many decades in the future. Eastwood doubly secures it, locking two sets of doors so that they can continue to *make their getaway.* To facilitate this, the two prisoners have to get from the sloping roof outside, onto the roof of the cable car and from there to the station floor before reboarding the cable car like normal fare-paying customers. By Eastwoodian standards it's incredibly straightforward, but Berkeley (Peter Barkworth) twists his ankle on landing. You see! I *told you it was dangerous.* For some reason this minor injury—more minor even than Burton's scratched hand—elicits a spontaneous outpouring of sympathy from Eastwood who dashes over to see if he's okay. In a film predicated on duplicity it's not surprising that Berkeley is feigning injury, writhing around like an Italian footballer back in the pre-Premiership days before all players, even honest, unskilled English ones, started going to ground at the slightest touch. Taking Eastwood by surprise, Christiansen jumps down from the cable car and gives him a good kicking, a foretaste of the kicking he'll receive a few years down the line at the feet of Scorpio in *Dirty Harry*, before paying him back in spades by stabbing, shooting, stamping on and generally fucking up his leg big-time. Having kicked Eastwood unconscious, Christiansen and Berkeley use him as a bargaining chip: they'll let him live if they're allowed to ride the cable car to freedom, a deal which Burton has no option but to accept, because if he doesn't we will be denied what is in many ways the climactic episode of the film, the pattern in the centre of its action-packed carpet in the same way that the car chase through the mountainous streets of San Francisco is central to *Bullitt*. As they leap aboard the cable car, Burton grabs an ice pick and dynamite from his infinite rucksack. It is impossible not to interpret this psycho-somethingly. So far, Eastwood has done almost all of the action stuff while Burton has done all the speechifying. It's as if his honour as a man, a Welshman, a descendant of the soldiers who belted out 'Men of Harlech' at Rorke's

Drift in *Zulu,* demands that he do something to show that he too can be an action hero, that he's not a middle-age alcy, that's he's not, as the saying goes, all mouth and no trouser (all hat and no cattle in Eastwood's western version of the expression). When push comes to shove, when Eastwood is down and out, when he's foolishly allowed himself to get stomped, he (Burton) will do something more daring than anything yet attempted by Clint—and with a fucked-up (kitten-scratched) hand to boot. Or maybe he's just a highly motivated ticket inspector: a pathologically determined cross between Bronson in *Death Wish* and Blakey from *On the Buses.* As the cable car begins its descent Burton finds himself, for the second time that day, clambering onto the cable car's cowling before clambering down from the cowling to the roof of the cable car as it sways over the giddy expanse of the valley.

The sound of all this clambering makes the fare-dodgers look up. You can see them thinking that most basic actorly thought, the one that takes us right back to the heyday of silent movies: 'Uh-oh.' The natural response to this, as Burton ties the dynamite to the roof of the cable car, is to shoot through the roof with East-wood's pistol, but after a couple of shots the pistol does what it's done so many times in the course of its long and complex history as a—possibly *the*—cinematic accessory: it jams. Either it jams or it runs out of bullets, just like East-wood's .44 Magnum at the beginning of *Dirty Harry*. No wonder Christiansen is angry and chucks it, like a kid throwing his toy gun out of the pram, into the yawning abyss. I should have pointed out that he wasn't the one hold-ing the pistol when they got into the cable car. Berkeley had it, but then Christiansen, in Burtonian mode, ordered him to hand it over. Now, with the useless gun not working, in that hunter-identifying-with-the-prey-type way, Christiansen seems to have taken on the chief characteristic of Burton and so, having ordered Berkeley to hand over the piece-of-shit gun, he orders him onto the cable car roof. Get him! It was Christiansen who suggested, back in the briefing, that instead of sneaking into the castle an easier way of silencing Carnaby would have been to send in a squadron of Lancasters, so he has some previous when it comes to getting other people to do his work for him. But so effectively has he channelled Burton that it no more occurs to Berkeley to say 'Why me?' or 'Get him yourself,' than it might have occurred to Eastwood to tell Burton to fetch his own fucking rucksack for once. So out he clambers, just as Burton had clambered on to the roof a few moments earlier, and all this *clambering* reminds us that there have been few moments when Eastwood has *clambered* on anything, either in this film or any of the subsequent ones. Only after his ribs have been busted by the kicking from Scorpio does he clamber over the fence at the Kezar stadium in *Dirty Harry*. Once his ribs are mended, he doesn't clamber onto the roof of the yellow school bus driven by Scorpio, he jumps on it and lands with the lightness of a panther, as he's done throughout this mission, with the grace of Darcey Bussell in winter combats. I said earlier that he and Burton *clambered* onto the cable car on their way up to the Schloss, but the clambering, I see now, must have emanated from Burton, who really has his hands full at this juncture because Berkeley has climbed up and out of the front of the car while, from the back, Christiansen has grabbed him by the foot. It's a wartime tug of war, and Burton is the rope. They're sort of *stretching* him until Burton does the only thing he can do in the circumstances: he kicks Christiansen in the teeth. Leaving aside all the killing, nothing seems more purely violent, more *Welshly* violent, than this kick in the teeth. Like the hand-to-hand combat you get in a pub car park in Port Talbot, it's actually foot-in-the-mouth combat. Shortly after finishing work on *Eagles*, Burton saw a picture in the newspaper of 'a Bobby being kicked in the face' during the antiwar demonstrations outside the American embassy in Grosvenor Square. Unsure where his sympathies lay, he noted that his own boys would soon be of an age to go on such marches, 'but if either of them kicked somebody in the face without provocation I would be constrained to kick him firmly in the behind.' Outnumbered two to one, fighting for his life on the roof of a cable car—provoked, in short, beyond endurance—the boys' dad plants his boot in Christiansen's two-faced face, smack in the cakehole.* It's nothing like as violent as the fight to the death near the end of *Saving Private Ryan,* but Christiansen's got such a gobful of boot that, having clambered up onto the roof, he must have been tempted to clamber right back down again to lick his wounds and survey the damage—severe—while poor Berkeley is still involved in a life-or-death struggle with Burton and his ice pick, both knowing that one or the other of them is going to get Trotsky'd before the ride is out, and all of us knowing that it's not going to be Burton. Having kicked Christiansen's teeth in, he now inflicts another grievous bit of harm: Burton drives the ice pick into Berkeley's arm, whereupon he, understandably, skulks back into the cable car while the other half of this high-altitude tag team, Christiansen, in spite of his extensive dental woes, resumes his

---

* Burton had been on the receiving end of a boot in the face himself, in real life. On New Year's Eve, 1968, he reflected on 'the legacy of that fight outside Paddington Station some seven years ago when my eye was so badly kicked by a winkle-pickered boot that I lost the conjunctiva and nearly lost the eye.'

attempts to pull Burton's leg. I put it like that, but it's no laughing matter, especially when he finds himself hanging on to Burton's legs while Burton hangs on to the ice pick hooked on to the cable car. First he's holding on to Burton's legs, then one leg and then just a boot so that one leg must be about six inches longer than the other and his arm and torso are probably stretched to the point where he's approaching the corporeal territory inhabited by his long and rangy costar. Eventually, in a way that will be familiar to viewers of *Cliffhanger,* Christiansen can hold on no longer and plunges to his death in what (Bob) Dylan (not Thomas) aptly called the valley below. Typically after a long and uncomfortable journey by car we get out and stretch, but Burton has to do the opposite, he has to *unstretch* himself like a length of perished rubber. Compared with the car's other occupant, who has suffered major ice-pick trauma to the upper arm, Burton is in good shape, and so, having unstretched himself, he wastes no time in activating the dynamite while he prepares for the most daring exploit in the whole film, one for which the recent limb extension seems like useful preparation: jumping from the roof of the descending cable car to the roof of the ascending one. It seems highly likely, in the circumstances, that some lines of Nietzsche's are crashing around his head. 'He who fights with monsters should look to it that he himself does not become a monster. And when you gaze long into an abyss the abyss also gazes into you.' No wonder we look at Mary Ure looking at him, looking into the abyss, which looks back at him and us, with our hearts in our collective cakeholes.

He makes the jump but barely makes it, the trusty ice pick just catching a rail on the roof, hanging on with his bullet-grazed hand before clambering up yet again, on to the much-clambered-on roof. He and we look back at the other cable car, whose sole occupant has decided that, while an ice pick in the upper arm would, in normal circumstances, be considered a terrible injury, by the high and bloody standards of the Schloss Adler he's actually come away almost unscathed. These consoling thoughts turn out to be his last—the cable car blows to smithereens without affecting in the slightest the one on which Burton perches like an avenging angel, a weary gargoyle who must feel that he has earned the right to spend the rest of his life quenching the thirst brought on by all this clambering, even though the real thirst—to prove himself the equal of Eastwood who, in the context of what in rugby is known as a ruck or a rolling maul, has revealed himself to be a bit of a pussy—has been thoroughly sated, especially when Eastwood groggily regains consciousness and asks Mary where the Major has got to. 'He's on the cable car,' she replies, which is tantamount, in this lofty context, to saying he's onstage, making his Oscar acceptance speech with a hard-on the size of a .44 Magnum.

After all this excitement, as Clint will famously phrase it (twice) in *Dirty Harry,* Burton is glad to be back in the relative safety of the cable-car terminal. Except that, in the language of the Schloss, 'after all this excitement' is exactly synonymous with 'before the next burst of excitement,' because the Germans, having broken through the first of two doors separating them from the terminal, are now pounding on the second. Unencumbered by hostages or prisoners—who, we can see in retrospect, were brought along only to meet their ends spectacularly rather than by cold-blooded execution—Cartwright-Jones, Mary and Eastwood join Burton in the cable car. Burton has only just got off the frigging cable car and already he's back in it again. He's become a commuter in permanently harried extremis. Behind them the door shivers on its metal timbers under the weight of blows from multiple sledgehammers. Down below, at the cable-car terminus in Werfen, the Germans have set up a machine gun to riddle the cable car with bullets. Not for the first time the Eagles find themselves between a rock and a hard place. To make the cable car less of a sitting duck Burton unscrews the two lightbulbs *with his bare, semi injured hands.* He is capable of anything now but has not renounced his old ability to give orders to Eastwood: set the bombs to go off in three and a half minutes! Then, in an allusive flashback to the opening sequence when they parachuted out of the plane, they line up to jump out of the cable car into a not-frozen—unBerryman'd—river or canal of unverified depth. Like drunk teenagers they've added a bit of tombstoning to their bucket list of achieved thrills. It might be on an altogether lower level of risk than fighting on and leaping between cable cars, but there is a serious danger of catching a chill as they drag themselves out of the icy water and on to the snowy banks. Passenger- and bulbless, the abandoned cable car is blasted by the waiting Germans before exploding, practically in their laps. Of the many modes of transport featured in the film few have done such sterling work, but life goes on and now it's the turn of the bus-with-snowplough waiting in the shed along with Heidi, who has had the motherly foresight to bring towels for her chilled and soggy charges.

Two of the defining* films of my childhood—*Where Eagles Dare* and *The Italian Job*—

---

* 'Defining' partly because there was, in a sense, so little competition. I can list on the fingers of two hands the films I saw on the big screen before I was about fifteen that were neither Walt Disney cartoons, Alistair MacLean adaptations (*Ice Station Zebra, Puppet on a Chain, The Satan Bug, When Eight Bells Toll*) nor feature-length versions of TV sitcoms (*Steptoe and Son, That Riviera Touch*) that my parents and I resorted to when it rained during our occasional, always dismal summer holidays in English seaside towns. These were *The Italian Job, Chitty Chitty Bang Bang, You Only Live Twice, The Dam Busters, The Battle of Britain, Operation Crossbow, Reach for the Sky, The Longest Day, Bullitt* and *2001: A Space Odyssey*.

feature buses, though the denouement of the latter is a cause for some uneasiness, since it cannot go unnoticed that the only black person in the film has, like many immigrants from the Caribbean, the relatively dull job of driving a bus (as opposed to the more glamorous task of putting one of the Minis through its paces) and he blows it, crashing through a barrier and leaving gang, gold, bus and audience tilting over a precipice of unresolved suspense. Putting aside the vexed question of race, the real reason that members of the self-styled Self-Preservation Society cannot be permitted to make their getaway is because they have been involved in a crime, whereas the Eagles have played a part in winning the Second World War, alongside their compatriots on other daring raids like Telemark, Navarone and *The Dirty Dozen* (both a caper and, in many ways, a thoroughly distasteful film).

It may have seemed fanciful to suggest that the jump from the cable car echoed the earlier drop from the plane, but the next thing we see is the very same plane from which that original jump was made. It's coming back over the mountains, for the rendezvous, the extraction, and it's done so in record time, making it all the way from an airstrip somewhere in England to the Bavarian Alps at twice the speed of Concorde.

Back on the ground, they're in the bus shed, the woodshed that's sort of a garage, with Burton at the wheel. He's simultaneously Neal Cassady *and* Ken Kesey, leaving Eastwood and the rest to choose their parts from the rest of the cast and crew of the Merry Pranksters. He ploughs straight through the door (why open something when you can smash it?), and they make their way out of town—FURTHER!— swerving through a parked row of motorbikes, a bit of vandalism which, though intended to impede the Germans' ability to give chase, also alerts them to the fact that there is something *to* chase. Eastwood and Mary blast away from the back of the bus, while Burton crashes through a barrier. They are outlaws now, freedom fighters opposed to the racist policies of the Third Reich, indifferent to any and all rules of the road except those mandated by the need to escape. Adam and Eve should have bolted from Eden like this, trashing the place and exiting at speed, leaving their Alpine paradise behind like a frosty ruin rather than skulking out, heads in hands, so that we would not be left, thousands of years later, harking back to some blissful condition of lost innocence and peace.

From *King Kong* until quite recently, the role of women in films was generally to swoon, scream, look threatened, be rescued and, ideally, get their kit off. Here, blonde Mary Ure blasts away with a machine gun like she's Gudrun Ensslin. Could it be, in fact, that this action-packed adventure is a premonitory account of the Red Army Faction's impending guerrilla war on the impregnable fortress of the German state apparatus with its concealed roots—all those twisting tunnels and corridors—in the National Socialist past? In keeping with this reading, although the concealed intention of the mission is to weed out top-ranking double agents, its most immediate consequence is murder and mayhem on a huge scale. Alarm bells are ringing, the entire town, the whole of the Reich, is on full alert. Eastwood has recovered so completely from the whupping he took back at the Schloss that he's able to saunter up the swaying bus towards Burton and utter the words that reawaken the old magic of their bromance: 'We've got company.' They've still got company even after Burton sashays in to the poles to ignite the explosives that are intended— ah, we understand now what they were doing earlier—to blow apart telegraph poles to impede their pursuers. Some still get through, and are in pursuit until a really big tree is blasted into the road, around which only a motorbike and sidecar can slither. Which makes one realize that although Adam and Eve were ordered out of paradise no one, neither god's minions nor the wily serpent, gave chase. So perhaps part of the eternal appeal of the chase and getaway is to add a crucial element of narrative propulsion to a tale of meek obedience—'Told to leave, they left!'—with all the attendant box-office drowsiness that entails.

The downed tree gives the Eagles sufficient time to do one of the things (strictly speaking one of two things) that cinema does best: blow up a bridge. Or prevent a bridge being blown up. *The Bridge on the River Kwai, The Bridge at Remagen, A Bridge Too Far . . .* Compared with these great bridges the one here is of such limited size and strategic importance as to be irrelevant, but since it's there it must be blown up and turned into that-which-is-not-bridge. Burton and Eastwood descend the slippery spars with one of the still-not-empty rucksacks and lay charges—but they're not the only ones blowing shit up: the Germans have managed to blast apart the tree that was in their way and blocking their path. They blow it apart so neatly that it looks like it's been sawn in half, but who cares? The point is that they're back in the game. Not that it's a game anyone in their right mind would want to get back into. The motorbike and sidecar gets to the bridge—there's the bus!—only to be met by a hail of bullets from Mary before anyone's even had a chance to say 'wir haben Besuch.'

Beneath the bridge Burton has fully reverted to type, snapping at Eastwood to set the rest of the explosives and then get out of here. By the time Eastwood has finished, Burton has started the bus and it's already moving off, so Eastwood, like Sinatra at the end of *Von Ryan's Express,* has to leg it to get aboard—except, unlike Sinatra, he makes it onto the bus and joins in the shooting, which is sort of joined in by the bridge, which explodes with an armoured car in its midst. Cinematically, the destruction of this bridge cannot rival the bridge blowing up in slow motion and falling away beneath horses and riders in *The Wild Bunch* (also released in 1969), but the effect is the same. Long accustomed to the convenience of a bridge, the surrounding landscape is left gawping at the suddenly enhanced power of the river, confronted by a complete lack of bridge. And spare a thought for Tamara Lukyanovna Torop, a construction engineer in the Red Army interviewed by Svetlana Alexievich for her book *The Unwomanly Face of War*. The daughter of an engineer, Tamara had loved bridges since childhood. In the course of the war she 'encountered hundreds of destroyed bridges, big and small,' and when she saw one 'felt about it as about a living being, not a strategic object . . . Whenever we went past the ruins, I always thought: how many years will it take to rebuild it all?'

Burton and his lawless posse are too preoccupied with how long it will take for their plane to arrive to concern themselves with such long-term questions. Still, with the bridge belly-up in the river, this part of the chase is effectively over, and we are faced with a contemplative lull. (If film stars had to worry about clearing up the mess they'd created, action movies would never get made in the first place and then where would we be? We'd be in *Celine and Julie Go Boating, A Sunday in the Country, Elvira Madigan,* or sitting through a double bill of *Claire's Knee* and *The Green Ray* as part of an Éric Rohmer retrospective in a tiny cinema in Paris on a Tuesday afternoon. We'd be in our twenties.) The bus ambles up to the snowy, idyllic, pre-rush-hour airfield and waits for the Junkers to appear. As soon as it has permission to land—rather nice, this return to the world of permission and order after all the anarchy and havoc let loose upon the world in the previous couple of hours—Burton veers off the road through the perimeter fence, dragging it behind the bus like a just-married car trailing tin cups and mugs, except this is such a massive length of fence it seems like he's pulling the entire perimeter with him. As if this bit of trespass were not enough, he starts ploughing into planes, which spontaneously explode. It seems wilful, but the idea is to stop the planes taking to the skies after them. Take out the control tower, he tells Mary and Eastwood, who also shoot up a lot of personnel carriers and generally lay waste to the airport like Palestinian fighters from the 1970s. The bus takes a curving approach to the waiting aircraft, meandering towards it like a river in a way that is reminiscent of how, at the end of a western, the lone cowboy, instead of heading straight out of town, always executes a 360-degree turn on his horse—a kind of equine donut—before riding off into the figurative sunset. Burton is the last man out of the bus and therefore the last man onto the plane, taking out a personnel carrier before joining the others who have scrambled aboard ahead of him, all of them conscious that space in the overhead bins is extremely limited, that without priority boarding you're going to end up jammed in a middle seat in the last row, right in front of the toilets. He should have thought of that when he had it written in his contract that he—not that cocksucker Eastwood—had to have the last word, that the last bullets fired in the film had to come from his gun. The plane, like cable car and bus before it, is riddled with bullets, but they're airborne. One can't help but feel that some vital component of the chase has been missed—vehicles charging along the runway trying to ram the plane as it tries to gain sufficient speed in order to take off—but we've probably had quite enough chasing for one feature, thank you.

It's all quiet in the noisy safety of the bullet-holed plane. They're sitting there while Patrick Wymark grades their homework, going through the notebooks with the names of all the top agents, the notebooks that were the real purpose of this extravagant undertaking, the notebooks that were in Burton's pocket when he jumped out of the cable car and into the icy canal but which have dried out quite well in the course of the energetic transfer to the airport. They went to all this trouble to get a list of names, so in some ways the mission is an allegory of the task of the film's producer and casting director: to get names like Burton, Eastwood and Ure on board. And they are on board now, safe and sound with all the names in the book. Except one. The name Burton wrote and showed to Colonel Kramer, the name of the top German agent in Britain. Your name, Colonel, says Burton. That's the thing with MacLean: there's always room for another twist, a twist that brings us to the most intriguing paradox of the film.

If Milton was of the devil's party without knowing it, then the writers, cast and crew of *Eagles* were secretly on the side of the Germans, whom they ostensibly outwit, terrorize and slay in vast numbers. Put another way, if the getaway is a spectacularly prophetic and triumphant allegory of Brexit, then the consequences and costs of that leave-taking are impossible to ignore. Everything in the film is German. It's practically an advert for the superiority of German manufacturing. They flew in and are now flying out on a Junkers Ju-52, tacitly endorsing Lufthansa's Frequent Flyer programme over BA's Executive Club. They wear German parkas and uniforms and have relied overwhelmingly on German weaponry (particularly the MP40 Schmeisser submachine gun). We have not seen a British weapon of World War Two vintage until now, when Wymark pulls a Sten on Burton. And guess what? It doesn't frigging work. This is perhaps to be expected of a weapon that was, in the opinion of Max Hastings, 'highly unreliable, prone to jamming, and inaccurate beyond thirty metres,' but, to be on the safe side, the firing pin's been removed by a suspicious Michael Hordern. When Wymark pulls the trigger the result is a dull, impotent, English click. Like Macbeth he is wielding a barren sceptre. We won the war, the film concedes, but lost the manufacturing peace. The point is underscored by Eastwood, who picks up his reliable Schmeisser and turns it on Wymark. *Vorsprung durch Technik!* Wymark has run out of moves, has nowhere to go except to England and a date with the hangman's noose which, if the Sten is anything to go by, might not be up to snuff either. Since the result would be slow strangulation rather than a swift snap of his neck, the prospect of serial malfunction offers only limited solace. That leaves him with one option, the option that opened up beneath Christiansen when he too was hanging—on to Burton's leg. The big drop that will lead to the big sleep. He opens the door, filling the plane with the noise of wind and sky, a Lear-jet howl of failure and having been found out, caught with his pants down and his fingers in the nation's cookie jar. Thoughts of Blunt, Philby, Burgess and Maclean—Donald not Alistair—flash through his head and then, offscreen (a surprising touch of Bresson?), he's gone, out of the door and into the void.

Now it's just the five of them. All things considered, it's gone swimmingly. You couldn't hope to come out of a five-a-side football game let alone a Welsh rugby match in better shape than this lot. They're just tired; it's been a long, often confusing, action-packed couple of days or hours, depending on how such things are reckoned. It's also been immensely profitable for everyone concerned. So it's understandable that they're ready to surrender to the soporific lure of the Junkers' engines, the monotonous throb making them feel drowsy, weighing their eyelids down, steeping their senses in forgetfulness, making them conscious—especially a Shakespearean like Burton—that our little life is rounded with a sleep.

After my book *Zona* came out in 2012, I was often
asked if I had considered writing about any film
other than Andrei Tarkovsky's *Stalker.* Absolutely not, I replied, consistently and truthfully.
That film occupied and continues to occupy a
unique place in my consciousness. My sense that
it is not just one of the greatest films ever made
but one of the great works of art of any time
was deepened by the experience of devoting a
whole book to it. And though it was, to repeat,
absolutely the only film to which such a book
could be devoted, I was aware of another, very
different, movie that made no claims to being a
work of art, which had an unshakeable hold on
me—'unshakeable' partly because I had no desire
to shake it off. If I were to write about another
film, I realized, it would be *Where Eagles Dare,* a
work bearing no trace of what Matthew Arnold
called 'high seriousness.' That must be why I
failed to include it among my pick of five films
as Guest Director at the Telluride Film Festival

in 2013, preferring to stick to the safer cultural high ground represented by the likes of Claire Denis's *Beau Travail*. Regret at having bottled it in this way increased when I discovered that *Eagles* could have been shown in a cinema at a ski resort high above the already high town, accessible by gondola. I made good that earlier failure of nerve a few years later when I introduced an open-air, ground-level screening at the festival, with snowy mountains and gondola in the background. The novelist Michael Ondaatje was there, and he turned out to be a fan, both of the film and of MacLean. For plenty of people, in fact, *Where Eagles Dare* retains an obdurate power and ageless magic. Steven Spielberg has cited it as his favourite war movie. In turn the *New Yorker* film critic Anthony Lane was nervous about seeing Spielberg's *Saving Private Ryan* lest it make him feel guilty about enjoying 'a work of art I revisit with the devout regularity that others reserve for the shrines of saints.' Considering that work to be 'the apex of a form,' Clive James, in a passage quoted earlier, writes of constantly rewatching *Eagles* to 'reinforce [his] stock of telling detail.' This little book is a narrative inventory of my own stock of details and observations, amassed over many years and multiple—if often partial—viewings.

Whereas I've never grown out of the film, the same can't be said with regard to the author of the screenplay and book. Alistair MacLean was the first writer whose work I read in its entirety. Before him I'd read lots of Beatrix Potter (my parents brought a book each time they visited during the week I spent in Battledown hospital having my tonsils and adenoids out), some Enid Blyton (*The Secret Seven* but not *The Famous Five*) and most of Richmal Crompton's *Just William* books. I'd not heard of MacLean when I bought *The Guns of Navarone*. His books must have been displayed prominently in the shop and the Fontana paperbacks had striking, identically formatted covers: photos (by an uncredited photographer) enacting what I guessed, correctly, were incidents or scenes from the books. The uniform livery encouraged readers to buy every book by the author. This I duly did, including the two originally published under the pen name Ian Stuart: *The Satan Bug* and *The Dark Crusader*. I especially liked the way that the latter began and ended with the same words: 'A small dusty man in a small dusty room.' That's how the narrator remembers his boss Colonel Raine (at the beginning) and that's how he leaves him lying there (dead, at the end). Some of MacLean's books were, I suppose, better than others, but the standard seemed consistently high. I blazed through them all without coming across a single dud. After I'd whizzed through the backlist I read the new ones in hardback, from the Hesters Way Library near my school, as soon as they were published: *Bear Island, The Way to Dusty Death.* I didn't read *Breakheart Pass,* which came out in 1974, by which time I would have been sixteen. So I must have outgrown him by the time I was about fourteen or fifteen. Initiated into this genre, I also read Desmond Bagley (similar covers) but didn't get round to Hammond Innes (with whom MacLean was sometimes compared). After that the only thriller I read, apart from those by hard-boiled stylists such as Raymond Chandler, was *The Day of the Jackal.*

Post-MacLean, or possibly overlapping with the tail end of my earlier enthusiasm, I moved on to the sword-and-sorcery novels of Michael

Moorcock featuring Dorian Hawkmoon and Elric of Melniboné (whose sword, Stormbringer, didn't just slice men up, it drank their souls). I was drawn to Moorcock because of his association with the space-rock band Hawkwind, who'd had a surprise hit with 'Silver Machine' when I was fourteen, and whom I saw play at Cheltenham Town Hall in 1974. After this brief foray into fantasy I began reading serious novels, started working hard at my homework, became a lover of literature.

I still have all my old MacLeans. Housed not on the open shelves alongside the McCarthys (Cormac, Mary) and McEwan, Ian, but relegated to a perfectly fitting archival box originally intended for Emerica skateboarding shoes, they're still in good condition, still appealing by virtue of those photographed scenarios on the covers: *H.M.S. Ulysses, South by Java Head, The Last Frontier, Night Without End, Fear Is the Key, The Golden Rendezvous, Ice Station Zebra, When Eight Bells Toll, Force 10 from Navarone, Puppet on a Chain.* Writing this book, I intended to exhume and reread a few of these titles to see what they were like, how they stood up to mature scrutiny.

I envisaged an appendix called something like 'Alistair MacLean: A Critical Re-evaluation,' but these few paragraphs are all that survive of that intention. The only good things about the books are the plots and the photos on the covers.

The pleasure afforded by those plots raises a more general point. In his book *Slight Exaggeration*, Adam Zagajewski writes that

> we can accept and experience narrative only once—we're not talking about Homer or Tolstoy—before it starts to bore us, weary us; the more sensational the narrative, the more wearisome it gets on the second reading, to say nothing of the third or fourth. One can imagine a sophisticated system of incarceration in which the punishment would consist of reading the same novels seven, eight, nine times—under the supervision of specially trained guards armed with glasses of tremendous optical strength.

The fact that I agree with every word of this and yet never weary of rewatching *Where Eagles Dare* suggests either that something about the nature of film as a medium renders it immune—or at least heightens its resistance—to Zagajewski's strictures, or that there is more to this particular film than its 'sensational' narrative. Or perhaps that the either/or construction is wrong and both these possibilities hold true.

The book *Where Eagles Dare,* however, is unreadably bad in spite of its narrative allure. To say it is badly written only addresses the surface difficulty, as it were. Did *adults* read this stuff or was I, as a second- and third-former at grammar school, firmly in the midst of the MacLean-buying demographic? *Where Eagles Dare* might be particularly bad because, in a reverse of the usual process of adaptation, it was a novelization of his original screenplay. That screenplay made such an impression on producer Elliott Kastner that he cabled MacLean to say: 'Best screenplay I have ever read stop adjectives useless to express my complete love of what you have created stop.' Entirely understandable, Kastner's abbreviated enthusiasm is easy to deduce from the edifice that was built from those original pages. A film script, Tarkovsky insisted, 'dies' in the film—but the film, of course, owes its life to that script.

And cinema, Tarkovsky reminds us, 'bears no essential relation to literature at all.' Appended to a book about a spellbinding piece of cinema, this brief history of my reading of MacLean's novels is a note explaining an absence, not an attempt to denigrate their author. It doesn't matter what you read when you're twelve or thirteen; getting into the habit of reading anything—of losing oneself in a book—is what's important. There's actually no *need* to reread MacLean because he and *Where Eagles Dare* are part of who I am. This book, therefore, is a chapter from an autobiography.

A third film occupies a formative place in my consciousness, in that autobiography. I first saw *Where Eagles Dare* as a boy in the 1960s, *Stalker* as an adult in the 1980s. If I were to attempt a third book about a film it would be about a movie sandwiched between these two (in terms both of decades and seriousness of intent), which I first saw as a student in the 1970s: John Boorman's *Point Blank*.

GD, California, September 2017

REFERENCES

p. 1: Martha Gellhorn, *The Face of War* (revised edition), London, Virago, 1986, p. 150.

p. 5: Elliott Kastner, quoted in *Movie Classics: Where Eagles Dare,* edited by Dave Worrall, London, Cinema Retro, 2012, p. 7.

p. 9: John Keegan, *The Second World War,* London, Hutchinson, 1989, p. 495.

p. 9: Max Hastings, *The Secret War,* New York, HarperCollins, 2016, pp. 254 and 257.

p. 11: Clive James, *Cultural Amnesia,* New York, Norton, 2007, p. 689.

p. 19: David Thomson, *The New Biographical Dictionary of Film* (sixth edition), New York, Knopf, p. 128.

p. 21: Thomas Bernhard, *Extinction,* London, Quartet, 1995, p. 317.

p. 28: Richard Burton, *The Richard Burton Diaries,* edited by Chris Williams, New Haven, Yale University Press, 2012, p. 399.

p. 41: Lt. Col. Dave Grossman, *On Killing* (revised edition), New York, Black Bay Books, 2009, p. 129.

p. 48: David Bruce, quoted in Hastings, *The Secret War,* p. 295.

p. 48: Alf Joint, quoted in Howard Hughes, *When Eagles Dared*, London, I. B. Tauris, 2012, p. 173.

p. 49: Don DeLillo, *White Noise*, New York, Viking, 1985, p. 141.

p. 49: Shirley Hazzard, *The Transit of Venus*, London, Macmillan, 1980, p. 75.

p. 51: actress in Hitchcock, quoted in François Truffaut, *Hitchcock* (revised edition), London, Faber, 2017, p. 65.

p. 58 (footnote): Burton, *Diaries*, p. 499.

p. 58: James, *Cultural Amnesia*, p. 691.

p. 69: Burton, *Diaries*, p. 201.

p. 76: Thomson, *New Biographical Dictionary of Film*, p. 43.

p. 80: James, *Cultural Amnesia*, p. 692.

p. 84: Elaine Scarry, *The Body in Pain*, Oxford, Oxford University Press, 1985, p. 63.

p. 85: Richard Ford, *Independence Day*, London, Harvill, 1995, p. 117.

p. 92: Burton, *Diaries*, p. 214.

p. 93 (footnote): Burton, *Diaries*, p. 246.

p. 95: Friedrich Nietzsche, *Beyond Good and Evil*, Harmondsworth, Penguin, 1973, p. 84.

p. 104: Svetlana Alexievich, *The Unwomanly Face of War*, London, Penguin, 2017, p. 172.

p. 108: Max Hastings, *Das Reich*, Basingstoke, Pan, 1993, p. 258.

p. 112: Anthony Lane, *Nobody's Perfect,* New York, Knopf, 2002, p. 241.

p. 116: Adam Zagajewski, *Slight Exaggeration,* New York, Farrar, Strauss and Giroux, 2017, p. 165.

p. 117: Kastner, quoted in *Movie Classics,* p. 6.

p. 118: Andrei Tarkovsky, *Sculpting in Time,* London, Bodley Head, 1986, p. 134.

Where Eagles Dare

UK Royal Gala Premiere: 22 January 1969

U.S. Opening: 12 March 1969

Metro-Goldwyn-Mayer

Brian G. Hutton	*Director*
Elliott Kastner	*Producer*
Alistair MacLean	*Screenwriter*
Ron Goodwin	*Soundtrack*
Arthur Ibbetson	*Cinematographer*
John Jympson	*Editor*
Alf Joint and Eddie Powell	*Principal stuntmen*

Cast

Richard Burton	*Major Smith*
Clint Eastwood	*Lieutenant Schaffer*
Mary Ure	*Mary Ellison*
Ingrid Pitt	*Heidi Schmidt*
Patrick Wymark	*Colonel Turner*
Michael Hordern	*Vice Admiral Rolland*
Robert Beatty	*General Carnaby*
Anton Diffring	*Standartenführer Kramer*
Ferdy Mayne	*Reichsmarschall Rosemeyer*
Derren Nesbitt	*Sturmbannführer Von Hapen*
Victor Beaumont	*Obersturmbannführer Weissner*
Donald Houston	*Captain Christiansen*
Peter Barkworth	*Captain Berkeley*
William Squire	*Captain Thomas*
Brook Williams	*Sergeant Harrod*
Neil McCarthy	*Sergeant MacPherson*

Printed in the United States
by Baker & Taylor Publisher Services